# Liberal Learning and the
# Great Christian Traditions

# Liberal Learning and the Great Christian Traditions

*edited by*

Gary W. Jenkins

*and*

Jonathan Yonan

PICKWICK *Publications* · Eugene, Oregon

LIBERAL LEARNING AND THE GREAT CHRISTIAN TRADITIONS

Pickwick Publications
An Imprint of Wipf and Stock Publishers
199 W. 8th Ave., Suite 3
Eugene, OR 97401

www.wipfandstock.com

ISBN 13: 978-1-62564-373-5

*Cataloguing-in-Publication Data*

Liberal learning and the great Christian traditions / edited by Gary W. Jenkins and Jonathan Yonan.

xviii + 150 p. ; 23 cm. Includes bibliographical references.

ISBN 13: 978-1-62564-373-5

1. Christian education—Philosophy. 2. Church and college. 3. Education, Higher—Religious aspects. I. Title.

BR115 L32 L45 2015

Manufactured in the U.S.A.                                                         07/07/2015

In appreciation, affection, and gratitude, we dedicate this book, *in memoriam,* to Stratford Caldecott.
*Requiem aeternam dona ei, Domine; et memoriam aeternam.*

ἀλλὰ καὶ ἐπιχειροῦντί τοι τοῖς καλοῖς καλὸν καὶ πάσχειν
ὅτι ἄν τῳ συμβῇ παθεῖν.

*{but it is noble to reach for noble ends,*
*no matter the outcome}*

—Plato, Phaedrus, 274a–b

# Contents

*Foreword* "Life and Learning" | ix
—*Stratford Caldecott*

*Acknowledgments* | xiii

*Contributors* | xv

*Introduction* A Christian "Mind" | 1
—*GaryW. Jenkins and Jonathan Yonan*

CHAPTER ONE
Liberal Education and the Orthodox Church | 11
—*James Carey*

CHAPTER TWO
A Catholic View of Life and Learning (in 25 Theses):
"The Glory of God is Man Fully Alive." | 30
—*R. J. Snell*

CHAPTER THREE
A Lutheran View of Life and Learning: Paradox as Paradigm | 50
—*Korey Maahs*

CHAPTER FOUR
A Reformed View of Life and Learning: Covenant Epistemology | 69
—*Esther Meek*

CHAPTER FIVE
An Anglican View of Life and Learning: Grace and Gratitude | 91
—*Ashley Null*

CHAPTER SIX
A Mennonite View of Life and Learning:
Practicing the Way of Jesus | 113
—*Sara Wenger Shenk*

CHAPTER SEVEN
A Methodist View of Life and Learning:
Conjoining Knowledge and Vital Piety | 124
—*W. Stephen Gunter*

*Epilogue* | 142
—Phillip Cary

# "Life and Learning"

*Stratford Caldecott*

EDUCATION IS IN CRISIS not merely because standards of literacy or mathematics have fallen, but because we have no coherent vision, as a society, of what education is for or what it is meant to achieve. We have assumed that, if it is not merely a cage to keep our young people off the streets, its purpose is to train workers in efficient running of the great economic machine, the machine that we hope will produce endless growth. But we cannot know what education is for, since we have no idea any longer what man is for, or what a human being actually is.

As Frank Sheed once put it: "This question of purpose is a point overlooked in most educational discussions, yet it is quite primary. How can you fit a man's mind for living if you do not know what the purpose of man's life is?"[1] We need a philosophy of life and learning based on an adequate "anthropology" or picture of man, if we are to put education back on the right track.

This crisis in our present educational system requires a response from across all the great spiritually-based traditions (I dislike the term "denominations") in our culture. We have to marshal all the sources of wisdom and inspiration if we are to meet the challenge. It is the religious traditions we must look to, because it is they that possess some sense of what education is for; what the human being is for. You could say that this is what they are for. The religious traditions exist to lead us to our true end, our happiness in God. All else is surely subordinate to that.

1. Frank J. Sheed, "Ground Plan for Catholic Education," http://www.catholicculture. org/culture/library/view.cfm?recnum=7367.

This is why the present book is so important. It is an attempt to learn what the great traditions of our civilization have to teach us about teaching, about education, about the purpose of man and how we may find the path we have lost.

For religion tells us we are both fallen and lost. It reminds us of the nature and purpose we have forgotten, the home we hanker for, the peace we seek with restless hearts. Education is not merely a training ground where we learn and teach the skills for acquiring more and yet more forbidden fruit. Rather, at its heart is the quest for ultimate happiness, the fulfillment of our nature. The word education means "leading out"—we may take this to mean a leading out from the shadows of Plato's cave into the light of reality, the light of the truth that sets us free.

Western civilization at its height defined humane learning in terms of what became known as the "Liberal Arts." These are the arts that set us free. Humane learning was an education for freedom. As described by St. Augustine and others, it consisted of seven fields of study, grouped as three arts of language and three cosmological arts. The first group or *Trivium* consisted of Grammar, Dialectic, and Rhetoric; the second, the *Quadrivium*, of Arithmetic, Geometry, Music and Astronomy. Both sets of arts were intended to be preparatory to the higher studies of Philosophy and Theology—that is, the love of Wisdom (*philo-sophia*) and the knowledge of God (*theo-logos*).

These Liberal Arts constituted the curriculum at the heart of the classical and medieval educational system. Of course, science has moved on since the Middle Ages. The world has changed dramatically. Nevertheless, the ancient categories are still important. In the case of the *Trivium*, even at a superficial level it is clear that the knowledge of how languages work, how to think clearly, and how to persuade others, are skills that are as relevant today as ever. Adding Latin and English grammar, and some training in the principles of logic and eloquence, not to mention some Great Books, to the curriculum of our modern schools would be a great idea. But the Trivium has much deeper foundations than this, as do the Liberal Arts in general.

"Grammar" goes to the very root of our existence, the source of our being. It is not just the rules of language, but the first gift of humanity, the connection to our Origin through memory, language, and tradition. I associate this with the Greek term *Mythos*, and the concept of telling stories to define our identity, or that of our nation and tribe. The word "grammar" was for a long time associated also with the making of magic, for with

Grammar we are dealing with the deepest roots of our existence. Adam naming the animals—and thereby ruling them—was the first Grammarian.

With Dialectic we move from *Mythos* to *Logos*, consciously searching for the reason of things. This is the art of discerning and uncovering the truth, of distinguishing between imagination and reality. Plato's dialogues mark the emergence of the dialectical method in its full scope, the transition from a poetic truth evoked or symbolically expressed by story and poetry into the clarity and precision of logical thought. But we need to maintain the link to the poetic consciousness—this is perhaps why Plato, even as he argued for the banishment of the artists, did so in artistic form, expressing himself through imaginative drama.

The third member of the *Trivium*, Rhetoric, has to do with the movement from *Mythos* and *Logos* to *Ethos*. Far from being concerned just with the rules of eloquence, it is about the communication of souls at the level of the heart ("heart speaks to heart"), and so with the creation of community. This is more than a matter of knowing the right words. It is the art of communion, of making harmony, of bringing disparate voices into one song. The truth or *Logos* of the world can be communicated only in love. And until it is communicated it is not completely known.

Thus the three arts of language consisted in the reminiscence of being through Grammar, the unveiling of truth through Dialectic, and the communication of understanding through Rhetoric. The subjects we choose to teach may be very different from those studied in the Middle Ages, but that is not important. The *Trivium* is about the foundations on which education is built, the deeper skills that make us human, the real skills our education is supposed to bring out in us.

Of course, we must also speak of the *Quadrivium*. These four subjects are not merely mathematical studies in contrast to the literary ones. If they were, we would merely be replicating the modern divorce of science from the humanities. They are about the continued search, on the basis just established, for the *Logos* or Intelligibility of things. Each member of the Quadrivium involves the study of patterns in space or time, leading to knowledge of the underlying Wisdom of the Creator expressed in the creation. This, of course, is the origin of the scientific enterprise, but it is equally the origin of art. Both are ways of discerning the *Logos*. Art exercises the imagination, and so in another way does science, where every major discovery has involved a creative leap. The artist searches for beauty, and so do the scientist and mathematician.

Beauty is the key to the lost unity of the curriculum, because beauty (according to the medieval philosophers) is one of the transcendental properties of being, that is, properties found in absolutely everything that exists. These properties include being, truth, goodness, and unity. Everything is true, good, and beautiful in some degree or in some respect. All that exists—because it gives itself, because it means something—is a kind of light. It reveals the nature of the thing and at the same time the nature of that which gives rise to the thing. Beauty is the radiance of the true and the good, and it is what attracts us to both.

The modern gulf between arts and sciences, not to mention that between faith and culture (driving God from the center to some out-of-the-way corner of the curriculum) is due to the fact that we have lost sight of these transcendental properties of being—and with them of Being itself. Reason has been reduced to discursive thinking. In order to bring reason and faith together again we must understand both differently, situating them in a richer, deeper, three-dimensional world. We must understand that faith is not blind, but is a light that enables us to see even the natural world more clearly. And we must understand that reason is naturally open to God and in need of God. If we close it off to the transcendent, we do violence to its nature.

If we do not know what education is actually for, our efforts to reform it will surely go amiss. It is the loss of an understanding of human nature and its flourishing that led to the present crisis. We have not been educating our humanity. The essays in this book do not all agree with each other, let alone with everything I have asserted above. But they all have something rich and interesting to say on the importance of faith, and the search for ultimate truth and human freedom through education.

# Acknowledgments

THIS BOOK'S LIFE BEGAN as a series of conversations, dialogues undertaken under the auspices of the Templeton Honors College at Eastern University. Each conversation began as a lecture delivered to the students and faculty of the Templeton Honors College, treating the Christian tradition of the lector and its stance as regards the liberal arts. There were eight of these lectures, and each was followed by an extended conversation with the speaker over dinner, at which faculty and students sat with our guests for the benefit that such conversations bring. The lectures as then given are not coterminus with the essays in this volume, as some of our authors were not the ones representing their traditions or churches for the lectures. But the lecture series was the book's genesis, and so the editors must begin our expressions of gratitude with Dr. Laura Hartley, now dean of College of Arts and Sciences, George Fox University, Newberg, Oregon, but then the associate dean of the Templeton Honors College, who worked tirelessly to organize the lectures. The editors wish also to thank Ms. Madeleine Stokes for her work in formatting and editing the manuscript. The editors also wish to express their gratitude to Eastern University for its support for the Honors College in its pursuit of the *ars bene vivendi*.

When thinking of our foreword, and then casting about for an author appropriate to our designs, a surfeit of candidates who had championed the liberal arts presented themselves to us. But in Stratford Caldecott we found one who had not only instructed the inquiring, schooled the unlettered, bolstered the faltering, and contended with the contradictions of the philistines, but a man who himself had internalized the liberal arts as habits of thought and action; that is, the *ars humanitatis* had formed and oriented his soul not just as having their ends in virtue, but their end in their very source, namely the Divine Life. Consequently, Stratford's love of liberal learning was of a piece with his love of God, and shaped the contours of his service to the Church. It should have been no surprise to us editors, then, that Stratford, though in failing health and a great deal of pain, agreed to grace us with a foreword to our volume. Yet his real gift to us was his life's work, which continues in the Centre for Faith and Culture, in its journal

*Second Spring*; and in the continued labors his wife Léonie and their daughter Tessa at the Centre. And we would be remiss not to mention his other daughters, the author Sophie, and the artist Rose-Marie, all as integral to Stratford's work as he was to it himself. Stratford's legacy comes to us as well in his numerous books, reviews, lectures, essays, and articles. Through his efforts, his clarity of vision, his elegance and logic, Stratford has marked out the paths for us to follow, trails well-marked to the True, the Beautiful, and the Good. His legacy is there to follow for we who now in faith, hope, and love wish to see more clearly what he now sees by sight, "l'amor che move il sole e l'altre stelle."

Gary Jenkins and Jonathan Yonan

Advent, 2014

# Contributors

- **Stratford Caldecott**, a graduate of Hertford College, Oxford, was co-director of the Centre for Faith & Culture in Oxford, and the G.K. Chesterton Research Fellow at St Benet's Hall, Oxford. He is the author of *The Radiance of Being* and other books, including a two-part study of the Liberal Arts: *Beauty for Truth's Sake* and *Beauty in the Word*.

- **James Carey** is a member of the faculty and former Dean of St. John's College, Santa Fe. He publishes in the history of philosophy. His book, *Natural Reason and Natural Law: An Assessment of the Straussian Criticisms of Thomas Aquinas*, is currently in review. His article "The Pleasure of Philosophizing and its Moral Foundation" recently appeared in *Interpretation—A Journal of Political Philosophy*.

- **Phillip S. Cary** is Professor of Philosophy at Eastern University, and Scholar in Residence at the Templeton Honors College. His publications include *Good News for Anxious Christians* (2010); *Jonah*, (Theological Commentary on the Bible, 2008); *Inner Grace: Augustine in the Traditions of Plato and Paul*, (2008); *Outward Signs: The Powerlessness of External Things in Augustine's Thought* (2008); and *Augustine's Invention of the Inner Self: The Legacy of a Christian Platonist* (2000).

- **W. Stephen Gunter** is Associate Dean for Methodist Studies; Research Professor of Evangelism and Wesleyan Studies at Duke University. His publications include: *The Limits of Love Divine* (1989); *The Quotable Mr. Wesley* (1999 and 2002); *Considering the Great Commission* (co-editor and contributor, 2004); and *Arminius and His "Declaration of Sentiments"* (2012).

- **Gary W. Jenkins** is the Van Gorden Professor in History and chair of the History Department, Eastern University. He publishes on Renaissance and Reformation intellectual history, including a monograph *John Jewel and the English National Church*. His current project has the working title *Tormentors of Calvin*.

- **Esther Lightcap Meek** is Professor of Philosophy at Geneva College, and among her many publications are *The Practices of a Healthy Church: Biblical Strategies for Vibrant Church Life and Ministry*, (1999); *Longing to Know: The Philosophy of Knowledge for Ordinary People* (2003); *Loving to Know: Introducing Covenant Epistemology* (2011); and *A Little Manual for Knowing* (2014).

- **Korey D. Maas** (DPhil, Oxford) is Assistant Professor of History at Hillsdale College in Hillsdale, Michigan. In addition to his publications in a variety of scholarly and popular journals, he is the author of *The Reformation and Robert Barnes* (2010); and co-editor of *Theologia et Apologia* (2007) and *Making the Case for Christianity* (2014).

- **Ashley Null** is the author of *Thomas Cranmer's Doctrine of Repentance: Renewing the Power to Love* (2000). Among his many posts and duties, he is a fellow of the Royal Historical Society and the Society of Antiquaries in London, currently holding a research post funded by the German Research Council at Humboldt University of Berlin, and a visiting fellow at the Divinity Faculty of Cambridge University and St. John's College, Durham University. His current project is editing the private theological notebooks of Thomas Cranmer.

- **Sara Wenger Shenk** has served as president of Anabaptist Mennonite Biblical Seminary (AMBS) since the fall 2010. Since coming to AMBS, she has overseen a "pivot of hope" program redesign, the hiring of seven new faculty, and a change of the seminary's name. A member of the faculty and administration of Eastern Mennonite Seminary in Harrisonburg, Virginia, for 15 years, Shenk has also held Mennonite Church conference and denominational leadership roles. Her book titles include *Thank You for Asking: Conversing with Young Adults about the Future Church* (2005) and *Anabaptist Ways of Knowing: A Conversation about Tradition-Based Critical Education* (2003).

- **R. J. Snell** is Professor of Philosophy at Eastern University and the Director of Philosophy Program. He is also co-Director, Agora Institute for Civic Virtue and the Common Good. He has published, inter alia, *The Perspective of Love: Natural Law in a New Mode* (forthcoming); *Authentic Cosmopolitanism: Love, Sin, and Grace in the Christian University*, with Steven D. Cone (2013); and *Through a Glass Darkly:*

*Bernard Lonergan and Richard Rorty on Knowing without a God's-Eye View* (2006).

- **Jonathan Yonan** (D.Phil, Oxford) is Dean of the Templeton Honors College, and associate Professor in History at Eastern University. He has published extensively on eighteenth-century religion, and is currently editing the journal of Christian Ignatius Latrobe.

# A Christian "Mind"

Gary Jenkins and Jonathan Yonan

IN 1994 HISTORIAN MARK Noll called a spade a spade. "The scandal of the evangelical mind," he declared, "is that there is not much of an evangelical mind."[1] This critique needs to be set against the backdrop of the widely held view among historians of Christianity that evangelicals, at least, since the era of the Wesleys, Whitefield, Wilberforce, and Zinzendorf, if not a half century earlier with the Hallesian pietists (Spenner and Francke), have been among the leading Christian social justice activists. The Hallesian Pietists asked about practical Christianity, about ortho-*praxis* and not just ortho-*doxy*. Their activism motivated them to organize charity schools, orphanages, and hospitals. And to be clear, evangelical pietists did this, not Enlightenment *philosophes*. In Halle it was Spenner not Leibnitz. The English evangelicals led the movement to end the British slave trade. It was Newton and Wilberforce who did this, not David Hume. To put it another way, it was not enlightened reason that gave the West its hospitals, orphanages, and charity schools. It was Christian love and Christian character (in these cases, embodied by evangelicals) that led these efforts.

So what Noll said in 1994 should not have been much of a surprise to us given the history which we already knew about evangelicalism. But it was somehow a surprise. It was a surprise that a card-carrying evangelical with scholarly credibility had the boldness to tell us the truth to our faces and to ask us to change. An evangelical myself, I (Jonathan) sometimes felt as I was reading Noll's book that he was diagnosing our special illness,

---

1. Noll, *Scandal*, 3.

1

not with a stethoscope, but with a scalpel. It hurt. In one place he notes devastatingly,

> despite dynamic success at a popular level, modern American evangelicals have failed notably in sustaining serious intellectual life. They have nourished millions of believers in the simple verities of the gospel but have largely abandoned the universities, the arts, and other realms of "high" culture.[2]

Of course, once the surprise wore off we found that Noll was probably onto something significant. Evangelicals are often constitutionally disinclined to the life of the mind, particularly as it works itself out over centuries in what we call tradition (what Noll calls a "mind").[3] In place of cultivating a rigorous intellectual tradition we have preferred an "activistic populist, pragmatic, and utilitarian" religion, as Noll put it.[4] By mind (or tradition), Noll means something like an accumulating and semi-authoritative discussion that has come down through the ages as a framework for thinking in the present generation. Such a framework can engage with all manner of subjects including ethics, politics, economics, the natural world, and the arts.

But many evangelicals are anti-traditionalists in that for them only the Bible, read in a present-minded mode, can speak with authority on any serious matter so that in Noll's sense there is not much of an evangelical mind. This has meant that much of evangelical thought has cut itself off from engaging the intellectual resources the past has left to us. Instead it has typically directed its attention toward future-oriented pragmatics of saving souls (apologetics, missions, youth ministry, medical missions) and caring for the needy (economic development, social work, non-profit management, counselling). It has also meant that our colleges and universities have struggled, sometimes fatally, to grasp their own purpose.[5]

What has followed over the last twenty years since *The Scandal* was published has been for evangelicals an intense time of self-examination. His book generated conferences, blogs, and a whole series of derivative books.[6] Many voices, usually within the academy, praised Noll's book; some quibbled with him on points; and a good number of evangelicals directly challenged

2. Ibid.

3. Ibid., 7.

4. Ibid., 12.

5. See Guelzo, "Course Corrections."

6. For example, Sider, *Scandal*; and Trueman, *Real Scandal*.

his conclusions usually in one or both of two areas: first, Noll's critique of creation science (see *Scandal*, Chapter 7) and, second, his observations about how the activist and emotivist impulses in evangelicalism have too often left little room for the life of the mind (see *Scandal*, pp. 46–49).

On this second point, in 2012, nearly twenty years after Noll's book first appeared, Janell Williams Paris penned a thoughtful and very personal article in *Christianity Today*, which in essence found that Noll's scandal was not much of a scandal for those who get what evangelicalism really is. "It's just fine that our intellectual life is limited,"[7] she comments, later adding:

> Instead of taking a tradition-building approach to intellectual life, I hope we evangelical scholars celebrate and deepen our current practices: teaching undergraduates, popularizing academic insights, working directly to change the world through service and applied research, and offering institutional and personal support to the small number of evangelical scholars who excel at theoretical and basic research.

Paris's article noted that there is a place for a small percentage of "evangelical scholars who excel at theoretical and basic research" to go on doing their work within the academy. They will be a minority within the secular academy because they are evangelicals. They will be a minority within the evangelical community because they do theoretical and basic research (in contrast to popular and practical research). Of course Paris's point is that what makes evangelicals distinctive is precisely the disinclination to study things for their own sakes. This is a point Noll fully grasped back in 1994, though he was critical of it.

For our own part, we see evidence for Paris's point every day in our lovely students at the Templeton Honors College at Eastern University, especially as they get started in their college careers. In one place, while reflecting on her days as a doctoral student, Paris summarizes the ambivalence that many of our students feel simply in being in college for four years.

> I hesitated, however, at the very notion of "the life of the mind" (I still do today). Evangelicalism had taught me that faith ought to matter in the world, and that Christians ought to address urgent needs through evangelism and interpersonal care. Does any believer have the right to live the life of the mind, I wondered, in a world where people are suffering?

7. Paris, "Service is Not a Scandal."

This sentiment is very familiar to us as Christian college professors, it is very burdensome for our students, and is something we try to relieve them of if only for their four years of college.

Then there is the subject of elitism. While Paris does not use the word evangelical subculture can be prone to see folks like Noll as guilty of this particular evangelical sin. As a group, evangelicals are not "shaping disciplines at the elite levels of theory," Paris writes, nor are they typically writing in "prestigious publication[s]." Paris does not suggest that it is wrong for Noll to do so (he is a well-published scholar at Notre Dame, after all). But evangelicalism, as Noll himself has pointed out, has a populist, democratic, everyman sort of religious temperament that is deeply ambivalent if not condemnatory of upper-class, Ivy League pomp and circumstance.[8] So, while few would call Noll an elitist, many young evangelicals feel discomfort in standing out for their intellectual achievement and will walk well clear of society's conferrals of prestige. This is a curious sentiment to say the least.

Allan Bloom's 1987 book, *The Closing of the American Mind*, received strong pushback from many in the secular academy. In response to this, the controversial William F. Buckley Jr. invited him as a guest on his television program *Firing Line*. As host Buckley opened the program with a sentence so apt that it bears repeating in this context, only with slight changes that make it apply to Noll's book: the special appeal of Noll's book derives precisely from the bizarre fact that it should be provocative to support philosophical and theological declarations once thought to be axiomatic among all Christians just a few centuries ago.[9]

It is, to use Buckley's word, bizarre that evangelical Christians should need to be persuaded (against our wills, it sometimes seems) to prioritize the life of the mind. And it is bizarre because this had been a priority in Christianity for the majority of its history. It is among other things what Christianity—including Protestant Christianity—contributed to the flourishing of the West. It is what created the culture that produced a Princeton or a Harvard or an Oxford whose original mottos were *Deī sub nūmine viget* (Under God's power she flourishes) *Veritas Christo et Ecclesiae* (Truth

8. Noll, *Scandal*, 59–81.

9. The program was taped on April 15, 1987 and Buckley originally said the following about Bloom's book: "Its special appeal derives precisely from the bizarre fact that it should be provocative to support philosophical declarations once thought to be axiomatic in a liberal society based on natural rights, to reaffirm the need for excellence, and to reaffirm the educational need to identify and, however circumspectly, to revere our intellectual patrimony."

for Christ and the Church), and *Dominus Illuminatio Mea* (The Lord is my light), respectively.

So what happened to evangelical Christianity? Noll's answer in *The Scandal* runs along the following historical lines. The Protestantism of Luther and Calvin (from which evangelicalism developed) argued for higher learning against populist anti-intellectuals who "expanded the attack on Roman Catholic dogma into an attack on education in general."[10] The Puritans, likewise, came to North America insisting on "a comprehensive engagement with learning." But in the eighteenth century a cultural shift took place within Protestant evangelicalism in large part due to the multiplication of revivalist movements.

Noll notes two key features of evangelical revivalism: first, the replacement of the traditional religious leader who derived authority from his place within the hierarchy of the institutional church with new religious leaders who derived authority from popular appeal. George Whitefield, Charles Finney, D. L. Moody, Billy Sunday, and Billy Graham are several examples of revival preachers who had a gift for proclaiming the faith in simple and accessible language and therefore attained immense public authority. The second feature was the way revivals, which were typically events outside of any formal church setting, elevated the autonomy of the individual believer over the authority of the church. The individual, though within a large audience, was alone with the preacher and was being called upon personally in his heart to make a decision and to do so immediately.[11]

When the political doctrine of separation of church and state is added to this mix, Noll sees a kind of tipping point. Whereas the revivalist dynamic tended to occur outside the context of the institutional church, once the national government refused to support a specific denomination all churches were in competition. "They were now compelled to compete for adherents, rather than being assigned responsibility for parishioners." Competition meant popular appeal, which meant the revivalist dynamic went mainstream and became typical of American evangelical church life. It became the norm within many independent, Pentecostal, Baptist, and other evangelical churches. It nurtured what Noll calls "a utilitarian apologetics" and a "functional theology." Churches came to teach what was likely to expand the church in a style that had mass appeal. After this, it would always be difficult to bring the life of the mind back into the church. Or as

10. Noll, *Scandal*, 59.

11. Ibid., 59–67.

Noll puts it, "the heavy pressure for results meant that very little time or energy was available to think about God and nature, God and society, God and beauty, or God and the shape of the human mind."[12]

J. I. Packer has framed the situation a little differently than Noll. His answer to why evangelicalism has tended to be anti-intellectual is that in evangelicalism, at least recently, there has been a profound lack of catechesis. This is how he has put the point:

> It has often been said that Christianity in North America is 3,000 miles wide and half an inch deep. Something similar is true, by all accounts, in Africa and Asia, and (I can testify to this) in Britain also. Worshipers in evangelical churches, from the very young to the very old, and particularly the youth and the twenty- and thirty-somethings, know far less about the Bible and the faith than one would hope and than they themselves need to know for holy living. This is because the teaching mode of Christian communication is out of fashion, and all the emphasis in sermons and small groups is laid on experience in its various aspects. [...] The well-being of Christianity worldwide for this twenty-first century directly depends, I am convinced, on the recovery of what has historically been called *catechesis*—that is, the ministry of systematically teaching people in and coming into our churches the sinew-truths that Christians live by, and the faithful, practical, consistent way for Christians to live by them. During the past three centuries, catechesis as defined has shrunk, even in evangelical churches, from an all-age project to instruction for children and in some cases has vanished altogether.[13]

Catechesis is the instruction of Christians into an entire system of faith and life. It is the process of rooting people into a tradition and installing them more and more over time into that framework of thinking and living. It seems that Noll has explained the historical roots of our situation and Packer has described one of the present manifestations of it. Evangelicals have programmatically and consistently turned away from theological instruction. The effect is a hugely theologically under-formed population of Christian people who no longer can think as Christians.

Many turned away from catechesis because it seemed irrelevant to practical matters of Christian life. But, of course, the whole idea of catechesis had always been about the formation of whole persons to inhabit a

---

12. Ibid., 66–67.

13. Packer, "What is the Future of Evangelicalism?"

coherent Christian view of the world: a preparation for life as a Christian in the world, not about ivory tower theological abstractions. For example, the turn away from catechesis has meant that many evangelicals have little basis for understanding the profound daily habit of repentance, of turning away from the old self and towards new life in Christ. Among the challenges that evangelicals now face is that lacking theological formation concerning repentance, too many are left only with some vague ethic of being true to the self. Getting right with God for many is the same as self-acceptance. But with a little more theological understanding, a doctrine of human fallenness, a definition of sin—any of these really—and one must question which self it is that should be accepted.

So we find ourselves—those of us who were not catechized and who lack any tradition—without the intellectual apparatus to think well. Dorothy Sayers once commented that without dogma, without creed, without catechesis, without tradition Christianity will be little more than "a little, mild, wishful thinking about ethical behaviour."[14]

The purpose of this book begins here. If we are committed to Christian liberal arts education our project is inherently political in that it has to do with the formation of persons to be citizens of some *polis*. Education, at least liberal arts education, is in this sense explicitly about the formation of citizens, which makes discussion of education, arguably, a sub-discipline of political philosophy, *inter alia*. Liberal arts education forms free persons (*i.e.* citizens) for the pursuit of the common good within the *polis* (the city). This is why this book is framed as a series of considerations about Christian life and learning. By life we mean to raise a broadly ethical and political question about the kind of persons and the kind of public space that each Christian tradition might have in mind. By learning we mean to raise a philosophical and pedagogical question about the sort of learning that best forms persons for such a life within such a society. But which city, we are compelled to ask, and which common good?

It is only fitting for teachers who are committed to Christian liberal learning to ask what sort of education frees persons for a distinctively Christian understanding of the good life, the question this volume attempts to address. To do this we have invited scholars from seven different historic traditions within Christianity to present a perspective on how their tradition might frame the purpose of Christian liberal arts education. The seven historic traditions are the Eastern Orthodox, Roman Catholic, Lutheran,

14. Sayers, *Creed or Chaos*, 47.

Mennonite, Reformed, Anglican, and Methodist. Taking an example we might ask, what is the city for which the Roman Catholic liberal arts college is preparing citizens? Or what is the city for which the Mennonite liberal arts college is preparing citizens? And so forth. Nearing the end of his book, Noll writes,

> the scandal of the evangelical mind seems to be that no mind arises from evangelicalism. Evangelicals who believe that God desires to be worshiped with thought as well as activity may well remain evangelicals, but they will find intellectual depth—a way of praising God through the mind—in ideas developed by confessional or mainline Protestants, Roman Catholics, or perhaps even the Eastern Orthodox.[15]

The majority of the following chapters arose as part of a lecture series sponsored by the Templeton Honors College (in 2010–2011) and jumping off from this point from Noll. Each contributor was asked to reflect upon two questions:

1. What is the distinctive vision of the good life and good society that is proper to your theological stream within the Christian tradition?

2. What sort of education liberates students to live such a life for such society?

These are by no means the only seven theological streams within Christianity. But in light of Noll's conclusions, it seemed essential to explore Christian liberal arts education by drawing upon the most developed resources available within the Christian tradition, and so the editors solicited these seven theological streams as the best equipped to engage wide-ranging cultural questions, including questions having to do with political philosophy and education, and why the book explores the confessional traditions that it does. As the most developed and most at home with the sort of questions that motivate this volume, the editors hoped to avoid superficial generalities on the one hand, and to find well-developed and theologically coherent positions about liberal arts education on the other. Each contributor has been asked to think only from within his or her tradition with no expectation for reconciling differences. The point in this is to allow the reader to have dedicated space to enter the theological imagination of

---

15. Noll, *Scandal*, 239.

each peculiar tradition and see it on its own terms. In this we hoped to attain a genuine kind of pluralism within this volume.

Instead of attempting to frame an idea of what an evangelical liberal arts college might be like (there are so many of them, and yet it is hard to know just what the purpose of such an institution is) we sought to provide for more focused reflection. Still while this volume tries to provide something of an alternative to the generalities that often come under the heading of evangelicalism, each contributor is nevertheless decidedly evangelical in cast of mind. By this we mean, in each contributor we have a person who thinks out of a different confessional tradition, yet for each one the tradition always serves the Gospel of Jesus Christ and not the other way around. Thus, far from surveying pompous traditionalisms, this volume rather gathers Christians who desire the reign of Jesus Christ, but who take historically differing, even disagreeing, intellectual approaches.

This volume concludes with an epilogue by Phillip Cary (by way of disclosure, an Anglican with Lutheran inclinations). Cary's epilogue fittingly culminates this project because by the end of this book, two things will be manifestly clear: first, that evangelicalism per se cannot keep erect its ship in navigating Christian liberal learning and that traditional and confessional Christianity must be called in for ballast; and second, that these confessional traditions do not agree in all places, which therefore underscores the need for ongoing conversation among these differing traditions as each part strives for the Kingdom of God. This is why Cary's thoughts on where conversation might go from here will be immensely valuable.

Finally, we cannot help but pause to express our gratitude for the late Stratford Caldecott, who contributed an elegant and fitting preface to this project, whose death cast a saddening shadow upon our efforts, but whose labors have done so much for the life of the mind and the reacquisition of our Christian humanist tradition. Our dedication of this volume to him *in memoriam* is only the least of our gratitude for a life too soon well spent.

# Bibliography

Guelzo, Allen C. "Course Corrections: Wither the Evangelical Colleges?" *Touchstone: A Journal of Mere Christianity,* 24, no. 3 (May/June 2011) http://www.touchstonemag.com/archives/article.php?id=24-03-029-f. Accessed, December 1, 2014.

Noll, Mark. *The Scandal of the Evangelical Mind.* Grand Rapids: Eerdmans, 1995.

Packer, J. I. "What is the Future of Evangelicalism?: Evangelicalism Now." *Modern Reformation* 17:6 (Nov/Dec 2008) 30.

Paris, Jenell Williams. "Service is Not a Scandal: Responding to Mark Noll," *Christianity Today* (January 10, 2012) http://www.christianitytoday.com/ct/2012/januaryweb-only/responding-to-mark-noll.html. Accessed December 1, 2014.

Sayers, Dorothy. *Creed or Chaos*. Manchester, NH: Sophia Institute Press, 1995.

Sider, Ron. *The Scandal of the Evangelical Conscience*. Grand Rapids: Baker, 2005.

Trueman, Carl. *The Real Scandal of the Evangelical Mind*. Chicago: Moody, 2011.

CHAPTER ONE

# Liberal Education and the Orthodox Church

*James Carey*

IN TRYING TO UNDERSTAND the relation between the liberal arts and a particular Christian tradition, we would do well to begin with a consideration of each member of the conjunction by itself, and then attempt to understand where the two might be in tension with each other and where they might complement each other.

Acquisition of the liberal arts is the aim of liberal education, which as the name implies has something to do with liberty or freedom. Liberal education presupposes leisure (Greek, *scholia*). Leisure has nothing to do with idleness, though the two are often confused in our time, perhaps more in America than elsewhere.[1] Liberal education presupposes that one is free from having to concentrate all one's attention on providing for the basic necessities of life. Liberal education is the education of a free human being. It not only presupposes freedom, but aims at it as well. It aims at liberating human beings from servile deference to unexamined opinions, including public opinion. Liberal education aims at replacing, to the extent possible, opinion with knowledge. And in areas where knowledge is only an unattainable ideal, liberal education aims at disclosing that fact as well. Early in the course of a liberal education one comes to know, in the strictest sense of that word, that one does not know as much as one thought one knew. One comes to know that some things have to be accepted on faith or on something resembling faith. This knowledge is not inconsequential.

1. On leisure in general, and the distinction between leisure and idleness in particular, cf. Pieper, *Leisure—The Basis of Culture*.

Liberal education originated in classical antiquity, in Greece. The speculative thought, the political traditions, and the artistic achievements of the ancient Greeks are constitutive of Western culture. The very ideal of science is of Greek origin. If those of us living in the West, or in regions of the world that are being shaped for better or worse by the West, wish to know who we are, we need to turn to the ancient Greeks, especially to the Greek philosophers. The Greek philosophers are of special interest to us because they know nothing of the Bible. Hence their thinking aims neither at advancing the cause of biblical religion nor at opposing it. The Greek philosophers have, one might say, no axe to grind. If one wishes to know how the world looks to unbiased and dispassionate reason, one could not do better than begin by turning to the Greek philosophers. The contemporary polemic against religion, against Christianity in particular, is essentially reactive. It is an exercise of neither unbiased nor dispassionate reason.

The liberal arts were traditionally numbered as seven and were divided into a group of three and a group of four. The *Trivium* comprised Logic, Grammar and Rhetoric. It was the precursor of the humanities. The *Quadrivium* comprised Arithmetic, Geometry, Music, and Astronomy. The last two can be understood as concrete applications of the former. Music considered the structure of diatonic order and its various modes, all the intervals of which, the tritone excepted, consisted of small whole number ratios until the introduction of even temperament in the Sixteenth Century. And astronomy, literally the law of the stars, considered the geometrical relationships exhibited in the various motions of the heavenly bodies. The liberal arts were traditionally understood to be, more than anything else, arts of reasoning.

Liberal education aims at the cultivation of reason, which arguably reaches its climax in philosophy, classically conceived as the endeavor to answer the deepest questions that human beings can pose to themselves: What is nature? What are motion, place, the infinite, and time? What are knowledge, being, the true, the good, and the beautiful? What is history, and does it have a meaning? What is the constitution of the world, what is its ultimate cause or causes, and what is our place within it? What is the best life for a human being? Does God exist? And, if so, what is His nature? Philosophy tries to answer these questions, or at least to attain as much clarity about them as is humanly possible. And it does this solely by appeal to reason and to ordinary human experience.

The Greek word that is frequently translated, and sometimes mis-translated, as "reason," is *logos*. Depending on the context, *logos* can also be translated as "word," "speech," "discourse," "relationship," "ratio," and "definition." The Pre-Socratic philosopher Heraclitus says, "We ought to follow what is common . . . but though the *logos* is common, the many live as though they had a private understanding."[2] And "Listening not to me but to the *logos*, it is wise to agree that all things are one."[3] The *logos* is not any man's private possession. Socrates enjoins his interlocutors to "follow the *logos*." [4] This formulation implies both that reason has an interest and orientation of its own and that we ought to adjust what is private in us to it. We should attempt to live rationally, which is not to say that we should give no weight at all to our private interests, only that we should refrain from acting on them when doing so would be acting in opposition to reason.

In Book VII of Plato's *Republic*, Socrates speaks of two kinds of rational procedure. One begins with hypotheses and, without calling them into question, syllogistically deduces conclusions from them. This is the general procedure of mathematics and it is part of the procedure of all sciences that rely on mathematics. The other mode of inquiry Socrates calls "the dialectical way" (*hē dialektikē methodos*), which could be also be translated as "the way through *logos*" (since *lek-* is the root of the work *legein*, "to speak," and, thereby, of *logos* as well). Both kinds of inquiry, the deductive and the dialectical, are rational or logical (*logistikoi*), for both eschew contradiction. But according to Socrates, the dialectical way is superior to the deductive. He says that, rather than taking hypotheses for granted, dialectic destroys (or cancels—*anairei*) them.[5] This initially puzzling statement of Socrates's becomes less puzzling when we consider how he converses. His interlocutor will advance a certain claim, frequently in the form of a definition, say, of piety, courage, moderation, justice, knowledge, or virtue.[6] Socrates will then lead his interlocutor to see that his definition includes the very term he is trying to define, or that it entails either a frank contradiction or a

2. Diels, *Fragmente der Vorsokratiker*, 151.

3. Ibid., frag. 50, 161.

4. Plato, *Phaedo* 107b7; *Republic* 394d9.

5. Plato, *Republic* 533c8. The word *anairein*, which can mean both "to lift up" or "raise" and "to annul" or "destroy," is the Greek antecedent of Hegel's *Aufhebung*, the act that drives the latter's own dialectic.

6. Such definitions are advanced and criticized in the dialogues *Euthyphro*, *Laches*, *Charmides*, *Republic*, *Theaetetus*, and *Meno*, respectively. There are similar exercises of dialectic in the other Platonic dialogues, and in Xenophon's dialogues as well.

claim that the interlocutor himself does not wish to make. Though dialectic can destroy a hypothesis by showing it to be untenable, it can also, albeit much more rarely and as a consequence of carefully ruling out all alternatives, deprive a hypothesis of its hypothetical status and elevate it to the level of a known truth.

Though dialectic is discursive, moving step by step, it culminates ideally in *noēsis*, in an act of the intellect (*nous*) that is not discursive but intuitive.[7] In this noetic apprehension, which alone counts for Socrates as knowledge in the strict sense, what is apprehended is "seen" by the intellect in its truth. What, on the other hand, is merely deduced from hypotheses—and, to repeat, this holds for all of mathematics, and hence for all inquiries that rely on mathematics—gets named "knowledge" by us, Socrates says, only out of habit (*dia to ethos*).[8] Because the conclusions of valid mathematical arguments follow necessarily, and often spectacularly, from their premises, one can be misled into thinking that the premises themselves must be true. But neither the validity of an argument, mathematical or otherwise, nor the truth of its conclusion, nor even both together, can establish the truth of its premises.[9] As for spatio-temporal, material, or physical entities, the concern of which is the only inquiry that gets called "science" today, Socrates says baldly that there is no knowledge, strictly speaking, of these things at all.[10] What he means is that generalizations from experience, which are characteristic of empirical science, are always characterized by some degree of epistemic uncertainty, however impressive the predictive and technological achievements to which they give rise.[11] Theories based on

7. Plato, *Republic* 511d 9.

8. Plato, *Republic* 533d6; 533b1–c6.

9. Consider the following argument: "All horses are tomatoes, and all tomatoes are mammals. Therefore all horses are mammals." The argument is valid, given the premises, and the conclusion is true. But the premises, both of them, are false. In arguments (particularly those of mathematics and natural science) that are more complex, that are governed by premises that are not manifestly false, and that also generate true conclusions, it is easier to commit the fallacy of inferring that their premises must themselves be true.

10. Plato, *Republic* 529b5–c1: "If someone, having gaped up (*anō kechēnōs*) or squinted down (*katō symmemynōs*), tries to learn something of sensible things, I say he would never learn it—for there is no knowledge (or science—*epistēmē*) of such things."

11. It is worth remembering that the, now generally discredited, geocentric astronomy of antiquity and the Middle Ages, as developed by Ptolemy and refined by his predecessors, was enormously successful at predicting eclipses and the like. Socrates's argument for a degree of residual uncertainty, however slight, in all generalizations from experience, and hence in all empirical science, is an anticipation of similar arguments by

such generalizations—and this includes all the theories of physics, chemistry, biology, psychology, sociology, and the like—invariably fall short of the epistemic accomplishments of mathematics, to say nothing of pure logic. For this reason, it should go without saying, though in fact it does not go without saying, empirical science is constitutionally incapable of definitively refuting the possibility of miracles in particular and the claims of revelation more generally. The scientist, or pseudo-scientist, who claims to possess such a refutation assumes, because he cannot so much as begin to prove, the absolute impossibility of divine omnipotence and sovereignty over the natural order of things. He begs the question, something he would not do were he liberally, rather than narrowly, educated.

Plato's student, Aristotle, recognizes that the *reductiones ad absurdum* achieved by Socratic dialectic presuppose certain indemonstrable principles, chief among them the principle of non-contradiction. According to Aristotle, this principle reflects the nature of being itself.[12] The same thing cannot both *belong to* something and *not* belong to it at the same time and in the same respect. Being itself, and not just consistent discourse, is, we might say, logical. If discourse is going to be meaningful it must adjust itself to this invariant aspect of being. As Aristotle sees it, a demonstration or a proof, when validly executed, yields knowledge, in the strict sense of the word, only if it proceeds from premises that are themselves known, indeed better known than the conclusions they generate.[13] If the premises of a given demonstration are themselves only the conclusions of other demonstrations, then either we are led into an infinite regress of demonstrations, in which we never attain knowledge in the strict sense of the word, or we arrive sooner or later at premises that are self-evident. The logical principles of non-contradiction, the excluded middle, and identity are, as Aristotle sees it, not demonstrable but self-evident. We cannot think of them as untrue because we cannot think without employing them.[14] And, indeed, Socrates employs these principles in his dialectic all the time, though he rarely makes them thematic. His dialectic would go nowhere without them.

---

later thinkers, such as David Hume and Karl Popper.

12. Aristotle, *Metaphysics* 1005b19.

13. Aristotle, *Posterior Analytics* 71b20–35; 100b5–17.

14. Aristotle advances a dialectical refutation of one who denies this principle, though he says that it can succeed only if this person will speak and mean something when he speaks. *Metaphysics* 1006a13.

Aristotle understands man to be the rational animal, the animal that uniquely possesses *logos*.[15] In defining man as the political animal,[16] he highlights the relation between man's possession of *logos* and his fitness for political life. Political life—unlike what takes place in animal herds, packs, swarms, and so forth—is characterized in great measure by rational discourse, or at least by an affectation of rational discourse. Political leaders give reasons, or try to give reasons, or pretend to give reasons, for the courses of action they advocate. And ordinary citizens do the same thing, all the time. Aristotle says that, in addition to bodily desires, there are desires that are peculiar to reason, desires that we do not share with non-rational animals. The desire to know, which Aristotle says man possesses by nature, is a desire peculiar to reason.[17] Reason as speculative has a natural desire for the truth. And the same reason as practical has a natural desire for the good. A sign of this is that we give reasons for why we think such and such is the case, and we give reasons for why such and such ought to be done.[18] To repeat, the Socratic injunction to "follow the *logos*" implies that *logos* has a teleological interest, desire, and motion of its own. It is not just a tool for calculation; reason is not merely instrumental.

In sum, though the word *logos* has a range of meanings, reason is a central one, if not the central one. Reason is that whereby we humans, uniquely among animals, are naturally led toward the true and toward the good. Thinking and acting that is not in accord with reason, thinking and acting that is inconsistent, is unworthy of human beings. Now, what does all this have to do with the Orthodox Church?

Until the Great Schism of 1054 the Orthodox Church and the Roman Catholic Church were one Church. They parted ways over differences that had been developing for centuries, chiefly regarding the procession of the Holy Spirit and the scope of Papal authority. And differences of comparable significance also arose concerning the meaning of original sin. These differences are well known, and I shall not add here to what has already been written about them. The Orthodox Church is sometimes called the Eastern Orthodox Church, because so many of its adherents live in Eastern Europe

15. *Nicomachean Ethics* 1098a3–5.

16. *Politics* 1253a3.

17. *Metaphysics* 980a22. See *De Anima* 432b5–8, where will (*hē boulēsis*) is said by Aristotle to be the appetitive part of the rational faculty (*ho logistikon*). Cf. ibid., 435a14.

18. We excuse the very young for actions we would not excuse in those who are older on the grounds that the former, unlike the latter, have not yet reached "the age of reason."

and Asia Minor. But many Orthodox Christians live in the West as well. There are a number of Orthodox jurisdictions associated with this or that country. Most of these are in communion with each other. They share an identical theology, and differences in liturgical practice are quite minor. The only significant point of contention among the different Orthodox jurisdictions turns on the vexed question of how Orthodoxy is best witnessed to the non-Orthodox.

The word "orthodox" is of Greek origin and is formed from two components: *ortho-* which means right or correct, and *doksa*, which in patristic Greek means glory, though in the classical period it also meant opinion or belief. Orthodoxy can be understood as both right belief and right glory, respectively right belief about God, or theology, and right glorification of God, especially in liturgical and ascetic practice and in the life of prayer. The Orthodox Church claims to possess the fullness of revealed truth. Unlike most Protestants, Orthodox Christians do not take Holy Scripture to be the only source for what a Christian is supposed to believe; Holy Tradition is given comparable weight. The Holy Spirit, who is called by Christ "the Spirit of Truth," is understood to guide the Church and protect her from error.[19] The Orthodox Church's claim to possess the fullness of revealed truth is a claim that goes against the grain of the egalitarian and increasingly relativistic ethos, or pathos, of the contemporary West. But Roman Catholicism makes a claim of comparable breadth, as do Judaism and Islam. As for the characteristic Protestant emphasis on *sola scriptura*, the claim that the fullness of revealed truth is to be found in, and only in, Holy Scripture, Orthodox Christians will join Roman Catholics in pointing out that it was the Church that determined the New Testament Canon. A number of texts, some of them frankly Gnostic, had their advocates for inclusion in the canon when it was being formed. That those texts are not in New Testament, and that the ones we are familiar with are in it, was the work of the Church. If the New Testament is divinely inspired, it must be the case that the Church was divinely inspired in determining what texts belonged in it, and what texts did not. The New Testament is, in fact, a product of the Church, whose founding predates that of any of the books of the New Testament.[20] The Church, through its leaders or bishops as guided

19. John 16:13. Cf. Acts 1:15—2:4. Note that the Holy Spirit is depicted as descending in tongues of fire on all the apostles equally, not as descending first upon Peter and then afterwards upon the other apostles (much less descending solely upon Peter and then flaming out from him to the other apostles).

20. Luke 24:45–49; Acts 1:4; 2:1–4.

by the Holy Spirit, is the authority for the correct interpretation of its own product, including passages in Scripture that can give rise to contradictory readings[21] and passages that appear to be in tension with each other.[22] The Church interprets Scripture in light of its own tradition, that is, in light of Holy Tradition, which was passed down orally, and not just in writing, from the Apostles.[23] The Church was originally understood to be Christianity itself: one could not be a Christian without being in the Church.[24] The Apostle Paul makes extraordinary claims for the Church in his Epistle to the Ephesians, where he strikingly speaks of it as the bride of Christ, yet more strikingly as the body of Christ, and most strikingly of all as "the fullness (*plērōma*) of him who fills all things in all."[25] In the Nicene Creed (more accurately the Nicene-Constantinopolitan Creed), which is normative for the Orthodox, Roman Catholic, Oriental, and Anglican churches, and for a number of other Protestant Churches as well, the believer professes belief not only in God the Father, Son, and Holy Spirit, but in the Church itself.

Unlike Roman Catholics, Orthodox Christians do not recognize any bishop as possessing a unique charism of infallibility. Instead, they place great weight on the doctrinal decrees and canonical decisions of the bishops assembled in the great Ecumenical Councils of the Church. The deliberation leading to these decrees and decisions was largely informed by the thinking of the Church Fathers, more than a few of whom were bishops themselves. Some of these men were well-schooled in the Greek classics. They were educated in the liberal arts. And though the Church Fathers fully appreciated man's need for divine revelation of salvific truths that transcend what can be discovered by natural reason, the most profound among them did not denigrate reason. They did not denigrate reason, because they did not denigrate man. They recognized, of course, that the nature of man was damaged by the Fall. Nonetheless they did not take the position that this catastrophe has rendered man totally depraved. They held instead to the view that came to be expressed, powerfully, in the Orthodox Funeral Service: "I

21. E.g., John 10:30, 14:28; John 6:51–58, 6:63 (cf. 1 Corinthians 11:29).

22. E.g., Romans 10:9, Matthew 7:21; Romans 3:28; Ephesians 2:8–9; Galatians 5:6; James 2:17–26; Romans 9:21–23; 1 Timothy 2:3–4; 2 Peter 3:9.

23. "So then, brethren, stand fast and hold onto the traditions that you were taught, whether through speech (*dia logou*) or [!] through our epistle." Paul clearly recognizes traditions that are oral, and he urges his brethren to hold fast to them and not only to the traditions that he has communicated through his epistles.

24. See "Christianity or The Church" by the New Martyr, Bishop Hilarion.

25. Ephesians 5:22–32 (cf. Revelation 19:7–9; 21:2); Ephesians 1:23.

am the image of Thine inexpressible glory, even though I bear the wounds of sin."[26] That the image of God, though besmirched by sin, remains the image of God nonetheless is captured in Christ's proclamation that we do to *him* whatsoever we do to the least of those among us.[27]

To understand how the Orthodox Church regards reason, we need to go all the way back to what God has revealed about the creation of man. In Genesis, we are told that God created heaven and earth by speaking. The expression, "And God said . . . ." (Septuagint: *Kai eipen ho theos . . .* ),[28] followed by a command in the third person, recurs in the description of what God did on each of the first five days of creation.[29] On the sixth day God speaks again, this time presumably to himself, saying, "Let us create man in our image, after our likeness." And, once creation is accomplished, God brings the animals before Adam and gives him the privilege of naming them, that is, of engaging in an act of *logos*. We can infer that this exercise of speech is possible only because Adam bears the image and likeness of God.

God is presented in the opening passages of Genesis as creating freely. He is not presented as compelled, either by a cause outside himself or by the necessity of his own nature, to create. Similarly, though his commands to his other creatures are irresistible, his command to Adam—that he not eat the fruit of the tree of the knowledge of good and evil—is resistible. Adam and Eve receive a command, and they disobey it. But their disobedience, terrible transgression that it is, is possible only because of their rationality, of which their free will is a component.[30] With his command God calls for

26. On the Orthodox understanding of original sin, see Ware, *The Orthodox Church*, excerpts of which can be found online at http://www.fatheralexander.org/booklets/english/history_timothy_ware_2.htm.

27. Matthew 25:35–45. See also 19:13–14, a difficult passage for those who think that humans are born guilty.

28. The Greek word *eipen* (with movable *nu*) is the second aorist of *legein*. The Septuagint translation (third century BC) of the Old Testament is normative for the Orthodox Church.

29. On the fifth day of creation, after God, using the third person plural, commands the animals of the water and the air to come into being, more precisely to fill the air and the waters, he explicitly blesses them; and then he commands them, this time in the second person plural, to be fruitful and multiply (Genesis 1:20–23). It is striking then, that on the sixth day, after commanding the earth to bring forth the land animals, God does not explicitly bless them (Genesis 1:24–26), though he does bless man (Genesis 1:28) and he blesses the seventh day as well (Genesis 2:3). The serpent is presumably one of the land animals.

30. Consider the formulation of Kant's, from the *Groundwork of the Metaphysics of Morals* Section 2: "Everything in nature works (*wirkt*) according to laws. Only a rational

an obedience that, as free, mirrors his free creation of the world. He freely creates, through love, a rational creature; and he commands a free and loving response from this creature. Had Adam and Eve obeyed God in love, they would have done so freely. Their disobedience was free as well, though, to be sure, only in the minimal sense of not being necessitated.

When we turn to the beginning of the *Gospel of John* we find that the word *logos* is prominent, to say the least. "In the beginning was the Logos, and the Logos was with (*pros*) God; and the Logos was God." Since we are told a few lines later that "all things were created through him," we can infer that there is a most intimate connection between God's creative speaking in *Genesis* and the divine Logos. And because the divine Logos becomes incarnate as a man, and not as some other creature, we have a further reason for thinking that it is chiefly if not exclusively by virtue of our human *logos*, or natural reason, that we bear the image of God.

If the *logos* that man possesses enables him to move naturally toward the true and the good, then how are we to understand the divine Logos that John tells us is with God and, moreover, is God. The divine Logos cannot be a movement toward the true and the good, for the divine Logos, as the second Person of the Holy Trinity and as God, is himself truth and goodness. Nonetheless, our *moving* toward the true and the good is an image of God, who *is* the true and the good, even if this moving of ours, which is *theosis*,[31] is never over and done with, but is, instead, an infinite progress toward God.

Our possession of *logos*, or reason, is not sufficient of itself to move us toward God. For that, the Incarnation of the Logos and all it involved has to elevate us toward God. And this elevation, again, can be resisted, precisely through an abuse of our reason. We should not forget that man is not the only creature in Genesis who can speak. The serpent speaks, and he reasons too, after a fashion. There is something about created, human, and finite *logos* that is able to resist its own proper vocation to move toward God.[32] This resistance, which is free and not compelled by man's nature or anything else, consists in his decision to follow the desires of his own heart rather than God's command. Man's rebellious disobedience is ac-

---

being has the ability to act (*handeln*) according to the idea (*Vorstellung*) of laws, i.e., according to principles, and thereby has he a will" (*Werke in Zehn Bänden*, ed. Wilhelm Weischedel, Darmstadt: Wissenschaftliche Buchgesellschaft, cf. *Critique of Practical Reason*, Book 1, §7 Corollary and Remark, in *Werke*, 6:142).

31. 2 Peter 1:4.

32. This theme is explored in Paul Valery's poem, "Ébauche d'un serpent."

complished though rationalizing, which is to say through self-deception. Human reason, though the image of divine reason, is not identical to divine reason. It is good, but it is not good without qualification. The only reason that is good without qualification is the divine reason.

Nonetheless, finite reason, in its natural interest in and orientation toward the true and the good, is still the acme of creation, in spite of its limited character and its capacity to be deformed into rationalizing and self-deception. And the Church Fathers recognized this. Consider, for example, the following passages.

From Irenaeus: "Man, being endowed with reason, and in this respect like to God, having been made free in his will, and with power over himself, is himself the cause to himself, that sometimes he becomes wheat, and sometimes chaff."[33]

From Basil: "Now, he has made us with the power to become like God, he let us be artisans of the likeness to God, so that the reward for the work would be ours. Thus we would not be like images made by a painter, lying inertly.... For I have that which is according to the image in being a rational being, but I become according to the likeness in becoming Christian."[34]

From Gregory of Nyssa: "Now since our Maker has bestowed upon our formation a certain Godlike grace, by implanting in his image the likeness of his own excellences, for this reason he gave, of his bounty, his other good gifts to human nature; but mind and reason we cannot strictly say that he gave, but that he imparted them, adding to the image the proper adornment of his own nature."[35] And, again from same saint, "While two natures—the Divine and incorporeal nature, and the irrational life of brutes— are separated from each other as extremes, human nature is the mean between them: for in the compound nature of man we may behold a part of each of the natures I have mentioned—of the Divine, the rational and intelligent element, which does not admit of the distinction of male and female; of the irrational, our bodily form and structure, divided into male and female.[36]

33. Irenaeus, *Against the Heresies*, Book 4, Chap. 4, paragraph 3. *The Ante Nicene Fathers*, 466.

34. Basil of Caesarea, *On the Human Condition*, translated by Nonna Verna Harrison, 44.

35. Gregory of Nyssa, "On the Making of Man," Ch. 9.1; Cf. Ch. 16.9 in Vol. V of *Nicene and Post-Nicene Fathers*.

36. Ibid., ch. 16.9; cf. ch. 29.8.

From Gregory of Nazianzus: "[R]eason receiving us in our desire for God, and in our sense of the impossibility of being without a leader and guide, and then making us apply ourselves to things visible and meeting with the things which have been since the beginning, does not stay its course even here . . . . Thus reason that proceeds from God, which is implanted in all from the beginning and is the first law in us and is bound up in all, leads us up to God through visible things."[37] Gregory is almost certainly alluding to the Apostle Paul's *Epistle to the Romans* 1:20: "For ever since the creation of the cosmos the invisible things of [God], namely, his eternal power and divinity, have been clearly perceived (*kathoratai*), being known (*nooumena*) in the things that are made, so that [those who in impiety and unrighteousness suppress the truth] are without out excuse."

From Gregory of Palamas, who, after speaking of Father, Son, and Holy Spirit, as respectively the supreme Intellect (*nous*), the *Logos*, and Love, notes an analogous relation within each of us: "Our intellect too, since it is created in the image of God, possesses the image of this highest love in the relation of the intellect to the knowledge that exists perpetually from it and in it, in that this love is from it and in it and proceeds from it together with the innermost *logos*. The insatiable desire of men for knowledge is a very clear indication of this even for those who are unable to perceive their innermost being."[38]

Now these passages from the saints, who associate our being made in the image of God with our reason, in no sense imply that our reason is adequate to ascend on its own power to the fullness of truth about God, though in the case of the passage cited from Gregory Nazianzus it is said that our reason can ascend at least to the knowledge of God's existence, as is implied also in the passage from the *Epistle to the Romans*. Moreover, these saints realize that we do not always reason rightly, and that reason can be enlisted in the service of the passions. But none of them would agree with David Hume that "Reason is, and ought only to be the slave of the passions,

37. Gregory of Nazianzus, "Second Theological Oration," *Nicene and Post Nicene Fathers, Second Series,* 204.

38. St. Gregory of Palamas, *The One Hundred and Fifty Chapters,* translation by Robert E. Sinkewicz, ch. 37, p. 123. (I have modified the Sinkewicz translation very slightly in the interest of greater literalness.) See chapters 33–36, for the context of the passage quoted above. In Chapter 39, Gregory says that "the intellectual and rational (*logikē*) nature of the [human] soul, alone possessing intellect, *logos*, and life-giving spirit, has alone been created in the image (*eikōn*) of God, more so even than the incorporeal angels." This image, he says, was not destroyed by the Fall, though the likeness (*homoiosis*) was rejected.

and can never pretend to any other office than to serve and obey them."[39] Again, reason is not merely instrumental.

From a consideration of the above passages from the saints, one would be led to expect that reason, rightly exercised, would rank, in the Orthodox view of man, near the top of man's natural attributes, though also in need of supernatural assistance from above. Or, rather, one would be led to expect that reason, rightly exercised, would rank at the very top of man's natural attributes, if speculative reason culminates in intellectual intuition (*noēsis*), and if the will is, or is an operation of, practical reason. But whereas reason did enjoy this rank in the view of the Church Fathers, it does not enjoy so high a rank in the view of many contemporary Orthodox thinkers, and it has not done so for some centuries.

The turning point in the Orthodox evaluation of reason has something to do with what happened at the Council of Florence in the Fifteenth Century. There the Greek participants were startled to hear their Latin counterparts argue for such things as the controversial *filioque* addition to Nicene Creed by appeal, not just to Patristic writers, but to Aristotelian claims about the nature of substance (Latin—*substantia*; Greek—*ousia*) and relations, and by appeal to the attempts of Thomas Aquinas to argue, on the basis of natural reason alone, that if the Holy Spirit proceeds from the Father, he must *necessarily* proceed from the Son as well, from both Father and Son as from one principle. The Greek theologians, arguing against the *filioque* clause almost exclusively from Scripture and Patristic sources, were not well-prepared to rebut arguments advanced, whether soundly or unsoundly, on the authority of Aristotle. Given that within a century after the Council of Florence, the West was thrown into turmoil, first by the Protestant Reformation, then shortly afterwards by challenges, advanced by philosophers such as Bacon, Hobbes, Descartes, and Spinoza, to Latin Scholasticism and Christianity more broadly, it became a feature of Orthodox apologetics to depreciate virtually the whole history of Western speculative thought from the time of the schism between Eastern and Western Christendom up to the Enlightenment and its aftermath as an aberration, under the epithet "Western Rationalism," without distinguishing sufficiently between what is rational in Western thought and what is irrational in Western thought.

---

39. Hume, *A Treatise of Human Nature*, 2.3.3. Socrates, Plato, and Aristotle would disagree with Hume's assessment of the office of reason. See my article "On the Pleasure of Philosophizing."

In particular, Thomas Aquinas gets faulted by Orthodox thinkers for trying to prove through reason what can come to us solely through divine revelation. But—without endorsing any of Thomas's claims here—it must be pointed out that he makes a sharp distinction between what he thinks we can demonstrate about God, which is actually quite a bit, namely, his existence, simplicity, goodness, infinity, omniscience, omnipotence, freedom, and providence, and what we can assent to only through faith, such as the Trinity, the temporal creation of the world, the Incarnation, the descent of the Holy Spirit at Pentecost, and the Sacraments of the Church. Concerning these latter things, which pertain to the articles of faith properly so-called, Thomas does think that reason has a role to play, namely, by demonstrating that these articles are eminently coherent and that they do not contradict themselves, or each other, or reason itself, or anything that we indubitably know. One can, to be sure, take issue, on the basis of reason, with some of Thomas's demonstrations. But he does not attempt to replace revelation with reason, or faith with knowledge. As he says, in a sentence worthy of the Optina Elders in nineteenth-century Russia, "Not one of the philosophers before the coming of Christ could with all their effort know as much about God and the things necessary for eternal life as after the coming Christ a poor old woman knows by faith."[40]

One might respond, however, that resorting to reason even if only to guard the claims of revelation from an appearance of incoherence is a suspect endeavor. But such reasoning was traditionally engaged in by Greek theologians as well as by Latin theologians. To cite just one example prior to the schism between East and West, Photius, in his criticism of the *filioque* clause and the arguments that Latin theologians were advancing in favor of it, engages in a reasoning that in its general style resembles that of Thomas Aquinas and arguably surpasses it in acuity and dialectical force.

Furthermore, in the dogmatic formulations of the pre-schism Church, especially in the Nicene Creed and the Chalcedonian definition, great care was taken to assure that what was professed was not self-contradictory. If,

---

40. Thomas Aquinas, *Commentary on the Apostles' Creed*, article 1:" Et hoc patet, quia nullus philosophorum ante adventum Christi cum toto conatu suo potuit tantum scire de Deo et de necessariis ad vitam aeternam, quantum post adventum Christi scit una vetula per fidem." Some Orthodox thinkers, in their critique of "Western rationalism," come close to equating the theological speculation of the Latin Scholastics, like Thomas Aquinas, who emphatically taught that human reason must be complemented, indeed perfected, by faith, with the philosophical speculation of men like Spinoza and Hegel, who argued that unassisted reason is capable of penetrating to the deepest truths of being.

*per impossibile*, reason had not been regarded by the Church Fathers as a canon they might have declared, against the diametrically opposed claims of the Arians and the Sabellians, that there is really only one God, but that there are really three Gods as well, and that God exists in three persons, but that these three persons are really just one person; or, against the diametrically opposed claims of the Nestorians and the Monophysites, that Christ is really only one person, but that he is really two persons as well, and that Christ really has two natures but that these are really just one nature. Instead of such nonsense the Church carefully taught that there is one God existing in a Trinity or Persons, and that Christ is one Person with two natures. In no sense were the revealed and mysterious truths concerning the Trinity and the Incarnation dissolved in the acid of human reason. But these truths were shown not to contradict human reason either.

Reason, being natural to human beings, cannot be dispensed with in our thinking, not even when we are thinking about faith.[41] After all, secular skeptics and radical fideists *argue* for their skepticism and fideism, if only by way of arguing against rationalism—whatever we are to make of their arguments. In fact, we cannot so much as begin to think, much less speak meaningfully, about anything without employing the logical principles of non-contradiction, of the excluded middle, and especially of identity, that is, the logical principle that a proposition remains identical to itself in its multiple iterations, though these three principles are usually identified and isolated for consideration only by those who philosophize. To be sure, reason construed as logic is not capable of directly proving very much of substance on its own. But it is capable of indirectly, or dialectically, disproving a good deal of nonsense. That many Orthodox Christians have come to take an interest in liberal education as classically conceived, that is, conceived as the cultivation of reason, is an encouraging development, given that much of the opposition to Christianity today is advanced in the name of reason. One can be certain that the Church Fathers would have argued that nothing that reason can definitively demonstrate contradicts, in the slightest, what God has revealed. And one can also be certain that they would be able to demonstrate dialectically that whatever it is that at bottom keeps people in our time from confessing Christ, it is not their reason, rightly functioning.

41. "[W]e must fit together, according to the explanation of Scripture and to that derived from reasoning, those statements concerning [man] which seem, by a kind of necessary sequence, to be opposed, so that our whole subject may be consistent in train of thought and in order" (Gregory of Nyssa, *On the Making of Man*, Introduction).

Liberal education culminates in philosophizing, an activity that goes beyond the practice of the liberal arts of the *Trivium* and *Quadrivium*. There is no way of knowing in advance where philosophizing will lead. The great philosophers disagree, and the history of philosophy is essentially the record of their disagreements, which we can make come to life for us if we carefully read and ponder what they have to say. One of the great disagreements concerns the scope of reason itself. Not all philosophers, but more than a handful of them, have concluded that human reason is not able to give fully evident and satisfying answers to the questions it naturally poses to itself. In coming to recognize its natural limits, reason becomes, or should become, open to the possibility of supernatural assistance, or revelation—given the absence of a definitive refutation of the possibility of revelation. But openness to the possibility of revelation, of some kind or other, though an important achievement of reason, is a far cry from faith. It is a particularly far cry from the faith of the Orthodox Church.

The faith of the Orthodox Church, though not a product of natural reason, nonetheless can claim to be a complement to natural reason, at three different levels: at the level of the good, at the level of the true, and at the level of the beautiful.

It is fundamental to revelation, as understood by all Christians, that sin is real and that love, primarily of God but also of one's neighbor, is good without qualification. Revelation in the Old Testament, most strikingly at Sinai, is in large measure the disclosure of a law or code of conduct. Christians believe that in the New Testament this law is fulfilled or completed. One is commanded to love one's neighbor, and if one suffers wrongdoing from him, one is commanded to forgive him. There is dangerous moment in praying the "Our Father." For in that prayer, we ask God to "forgive us our debts, as (*hōs*) we forgive our debtors." If we do not forgive our debtors we are, in this prayer, effectively asking God not to forgive us. Hence Orthodox teaching is that one be sure to have forgiven one's debtors before saying this prayer. And, of course, love of one's neighbor is extended by Christ's command to love even one's enemies. One is commanded to work, when possible, for their moral and spiritual welfare, and to pray for them, which is always possible. This command accords with the fact that all human beings are, by virtue of their reason and free will, made in the image of God, and that the image of God in them is worthy of awe, respect, and love, even when fouled by sin. The very fact that man has to be commanded to love, it has been aptly noted, is evidence of his sinful nature. Christ's command contributes to the perfection of practical reason by elevating the individual human being out of his irrational self-absorption and his equally irrational proclivity to regard the world solely as it revolves around him as all there is to the world.[42]

Essential to revelation, as understood by most Christians, are certain theological truths, such as the Trinity and the Incarnation. I say "most Christians" and not "all Christians," because theology is held in suspicion in certain quarters these days.[43] Theological distinctions give rise to theological divisions, and thereby, alas, to varying degrees of animosity. It is increasingly said that one does not need theology, literally, *logos* or reason regarding God: one needs only to love Jesus and confess that he is the Lord. The problem with this formulation, however, is that one has to *mean* something in confessing that Jesus is the Lord. Is one confessing that he is God simply? Or that he is a man simply? Or that he is partly God and partly man, a kind of hybrid that is neither fully God nor fully man? And how is Jesus related to his Father? Are they one and the same person, just appearing to the world in different ways? Or are they, along with the Holy Spirit, actually three gods? These questions have been answered, coherently and consistently, by the Church Fathers, both in theological treatises and in the dogmatic decrees of the Ecumenical Councils. Christianity, as a religion in which faith as distinct from observance is primary, is essentially theological. And theology is omnipresent in the Orthodox Church, not only in the recitation of the Nicene Creed but also in the Church's hymnody, canons, and icons as well, and in the priest's homilies. Revealed theology presents speculative reason with claims that it could not arrive at on its own. To the believer, these claims make sense of the world, its ultimate foundation, and his place in it, in a way that no other claims, including those of natural science and psychology, are able to.

Distinctive of the Orthodox Church is the centrality of beauty. As Fr. Alexander Elchaninov, a twentieth-century Russian priest, said, "Orthodoxy is Christianity understood as supreme Beauty." Whereas the good and the true are the concern of practical and speculative reason, respectively, the beautiful is the concern of incarnate reason, that is, of man as both rational and animal.[44] The centrality of beauty in the Orthodox Church is in-

42. On the "touching of other worlds," see Dostoyevsky, *The Brothers Karamazov.*

43. It suffices to think in this connection of the recent proliferation of Christian communities that pride themselves on being "non-denominational," which is to say, more clearly than anything else, non-theological.

44. Carey, "Aesthetics, Ancient and Modern."

separable from the Orthodox understanding of the Incarnation, according to which God would have become man even if Adam and Eve had never sinned. For the ultimate end of man was not simply to tend the garden of Eden without sin, but to become an actual partaker of the divine nature.[45] This end is, to be sure, never fully attained. Movement toward it, however, initiated in this life and continued in the next, is the process of divinization, or *theosis*. Icons of the saints, including icons of the Virgin Mary, whom Orthodox call the Theotokos (the one who bore God), depict *theosis*. In the icons of Christ the attempt is not to depict man in the process of *becoming* divine, but to depict God *having become* man. Though Christianity is commonly criticized for despising the body, the criticism is way off target. There is no other religion in which the body is accorded higher dignity. And this is especially true in the Orthodox Church, with its emphasis on the Incarnation, on the sacraments, and on the resurrection of the body (as distinct from immortality of the soul merely). Moreover, Christ is understood, in his glorious Ascension, to have taken his body and his whole human nature, which he received from his mother, right into the bosom of the Trinity: Consequent to Christ's Ascension, the very Godhead contains a human body, and will contain it for all eternity.

The Orthodox Church then teaches that the Incarnation, Resurrection, and Ascension of Christ has endowed the physical world with a dignity it otherwise would never have had. Physical beauty is the effect of the radiance of the divine into the world. The Orthodox Church strives in its icons and hymnody, and in the solemnity and sobriety of its services, to acknowledge this radiance. There is no desire to bring either the Church's teachings or its liturgical practice into accord with contemporary tastes. There are no "rock" bands in the services of the Orthodox Church (nor any other instrumental music for that matter), the priests do not make jokes in their homilies, there is no "Christian rap," and there are no clown masses.

Human reason, which is discursive, has as its goal an intellectual-intuitive, or noetic, apprehension of the truth. The Apostle Paul says that "now we see through a glass darkly; but then face to face." This "seeing face to face," or person to person, is the theological transformation of the philosophical conception of *noēsis*. The ultimate experience of truth is the personal experience, not of a proposition or a formal principle, but of God himself as a Trinity of persons united by love.[46] The Orthodox Church,

---

45. Cf. note 31.

46. John 14:6; 1 John 4:8, 16.

devoting itself to "Christianity as supreme Beauty" gives the believer a fore-taste of the noetic encounter with God. In so doing, it in no way repudiates liberal education or the liberal arts. But it does leave them far behind. It leaves them very far behind.

## Bibliography

Aristotle. *Basic Works*. Edited with introduction by Richard McKeon. Translated by E. M. Edghill, et al. New York: Random House, 1966.

Basil of Caesarea. *On the Human Condition*. Translated by Nonna Verna Harrison. Crestwood: St. Vladimir's Seminary Press, 2005.

Carey, James. "Aesthetics, Ancient and Modern: An Introduction." *St. John's Review* 53:2 (Fall 2012) 1–37.

———. "On the Pleasure of Philosophizing and its Moral Foundation." *Interpretation—A Journal of Political Philosophy* 40:2 (Fall) 253.

Diels, Hermann. *Die Fragmente der Vorsokratiker*. Berlin: Weidmann, 1935.

Dostoyevsky, Fyodor. *The Brothers Karamazov*. Translated by Richard Pevear and Larissa Volokhonsky. 12th edition. New York: Farrar, Straus and Giroux, 2002.

Gregory of Palamas. *The One Hundred and Fifty Chapters*. Edited and translated by Robert E. Sinkewicz. Toronto: Pontifical Institute of Medieval Studies, 1988.

Hume, David. *A Treatise of Human Nature*. Oxford: Oxford University Press, 2000.

Kant, Immanuel. *Werke in Zehn Bänden*. Edited by Wilhelm Weischedel. Darmstadt: Wissenschaftliche Buchgesellschaft, 2011.

Pieper, Josef. *Leisure—The Basis of Culture*. Translated by Alexander Dru with introduction by T. S. Eliot. New York: Pantheon, 1952.

Plato. *Complete Works*. Edited by John Cooper. Translated by G. M. A. Grube et al. Indianapolis: Hackett, 1997.

Schaff, Philip, et al. *The Ante Nicene Fathers*. Grand Rapids: Hendrickson, 1996.

———. *Nicene and Post Nicene Fathers, Second Series*. Grand Rapids: Hendrickson, 1996.

Thomas Aquinas. "Commentary on the Apostles' Creed." In *The Three Greatest Prayers: Commentaries on the Lord's Prayer, the Hail Mary, and the Apostle's Creed*. Translated by Laurence Shapcote. Manchester, NH: Sophia Institute Press, 1990.

Troitsky, Bishop Hilarion. "Christianity or The Church." Orthodox Info. (No Date) http://orthodoxinfo.com/inquirers/ sthilarion_church.aspx. Accessed December 1, 2014.

Ware Timothy (later, Bishop Kallistos). *The Orthodox Church*. New York: Penguin, 1993.

# CHAPTER TWO

# A Catholic View of Life
# and Learning (in 25 Theses):
# "The Glory of God is
# Man Fully Alive"

*R. J. Snell*

## Goodness and Contemplation

1. God is an eternal communion of three persons. As communion, the "very inner life of God himself, the supreme fullness of what it means to be, is by its very nature *self-communicative Love*."[1] The Father communicates his divine nature fully to the Son and "both, together, in a single act of mutual love, pour forth the same divine essence again in all its fullness" to the Holy Spirit.[2] Ecstatic communication subsequently, although freely, without any necessity, flows into creation and self-communication is etched deeply into the meaning and structure of existence. *To be* is more than facticity, it is "to be *actively present*."[3] Thus, all that is, in its own way, seeks its own perfection or actuality which is intrinsically relational and communicative.

2. Given the personal meaning of all reality, "at every time and in every place, God draws close to man. He calls man to seek him, to know

1. Clarke, *Person and Being*, 11.
2. Ibid., 12.
3. Ibid., 13.

him, to love him with all his strength"—God seeks always to communicate Himself.[4]

> God, who through the Word creates all things (see John 1:3) and keeps them in existence, gives men an enduring witness to Himself in created realities (see Rom. 1:19-20). Planning to make known the way of heavenly salvation, He went further and from the start manifested Himself to our first parents. Then after their fall His promise of redemption aroused in them the hope of being saved (see Gen. 3:15) and from that time on He ceaselessly kept the human race in His care. . . . [5]

In His goodness, God makes Himself known throughout salvation history, culminating in the definitive revelation of Jesus Christ through whom God, "out of the abundance of His love speaks to men as friends . . . and lives among them" so that "man might . . . have access to the Father and come to share in the divine nature," entering into "fellowship with Himself."[6] Consequently, the "Redeemer of man, Jesus Christ, is the center of the universe and of history," as well as the grounds of meaning and dignity for every person, endeavour, act, study, or institution.[7]

3. Ontologically—as the one through whom all things were made—and epistemologically—as the definitive Image and revelation of the Father—the ground of all creation is God in Christ. As such, the worth of all creation is a non-necessary gift. Contingent things, by definition, need not be but are entirely and utterly dependent for their being, a dependence which establishes rather than diminishes their worth. As dependent on the free gift of God, things are "no longer *pragmata or chrêmata*, or even merely *onta*; they are *creaturae*, creatures under the 'Great Economy' of God."[8] God need not have made them, nor are they self-sustaining, but dependent, meaning that "if the universe is the gift of the person of God, it follows that it is not indifferent to persons and their values . . . the very character and status of things will reflect their giftedness in their radical contingency and the received

---

4. *Catechism of the Catholic Church,* 1.

5. *Dei Verbum,* 3.

6. Ibid., 2.

7. John Paul II, *Redemptor Hominis,* 1.

8. Schmitz, *Recovery of Wonder,* 29.

generosity inherent in them."[9] That is, because creation depends on the generous and ecstatic outpouring of God's communion, all creation carries and speaks this generosity in itself, and in a particular way the human person:

> The dignity of man rests above all on the fact that he is called to communion with God. This invitation to converse with God is addressed to man as soon as he comes into being. For if man exists, it is because God has created him through love, and through love continues to hold him in existence. He cannot live fully according to truth unless he freely acknowledges that love and entrusts himself to his creator.[10]

4. While dependent for dignity and value, nothing human is thereby diminished. Not only does God will all creation to be, but also to be good, containing its due and proper perfection. *"Et vidit Deus quod esset bonum."* And God saw that it was good (Gen 1:10). Further, while all that is is good, "the life which God gives man is quite different from the life of all other living creatures, inasmuch as man, although formed from the dust of the earth . . . *is a manifestation of God in the world, a sign of his presence, a trace of his glory."*[11] Of all creation, only the person is willed for their own sake, and there is a deep amazement at the "wonder" which is every human person.[12] Since God is transcendent, there can be no competition between God and the person, no tension between God's sovereignty and human freedom, no zero-sum between the dignity of God and persons or between the glory of God and the majesty of the human created in the very image of God. In fact, the glory of God is the person fully alive—*Gloria Dei vivens homo!*[13] To seek the flourishing of the human in keeping with their integral development, in part, is to glorify God, and so every genuine advance in human integrity, well-being, progress, or self-constitution is service to God and a work of prayer:

> Thus, far from thinking that works produced by man's own talent and energy are in opposition to God's power, and that

---

9. Ibid., 31; cf. Gilson, *Spirit of Mediaeval Philosophy*, 128–47.

10. *Guadium et Spes*, 19.

11. John Paul II, *Evangelium Vitae*, 34.

12. Ibid., 83.

13. Ibid., 34, referencing St. Irenaeus.

the rational creature exists as a kind of rival to the Creator, Christians are convinced that the triumphs of the human race are a sign of God's grace and the flowering of His own mysterious design.[14]

Christianity is a humanism, then, "*an integral and solidary humanism,*"[15] for God despises nothing He has made (Wis 11:24). In fact, "the name for that deep amazement at man's worth and dignity is the Gospel, that is to say: the Good News. It is also called Christianity."[16]

5. The fundamental goodness of creation and the value of the human person is definitively reaffirmed, even as perfected and elevated, by the Incarnation and redemptive work of Jesus Christ, the Second Adam: "In him has been revealed in a new and more wonderful way the fundamental truth concerning creation to which the Book of Genesis gives witness when it repeats several times: 'God saw that it was good.'"[17] The futility of sin is overcome as the world "recovers again its original link with the divine source of Wisdom and Love . . . . As this link was broken in the man Adam, so in the Man Christ it was reforged."[18] Rather than subverting or replacing the natural human vocation, the new Adam "*fully reveals man to himself* and brings to light his most high calling . . . . Human nature, by the very fact that it was assumed, not absorbed, in him, has been raised in us also to a dignity beyond compare."[19] God's original joy and affirmation in the goodness of creation is affirmed in an unfathomably excessive way, for rather than merely healing creation, He joins it, He becomes it, He takes it on, and in so doing God "*in a certain way united himself with each man.*"[20] For Christ plays in ten thousand places now, and wombs and mangers, workshops and tables, dusty streets and sandals, bread and wine, and, indeed, every person and their work, is now a sacrament of sorts, a bearer of the divine.

14. *Guadium et Spes*, 34.

15. *Compendium of Social Doctrine*, 19.

16. John Paul II, *Redemptor Hominis*, 10.

17. Ibid., 8.

18. Ibid.

19. Ibid., 10.

20. Ibid.

6. "He worked with human hands, he thought with a human mind. He acted with a human will, and with a human heart he loved. Born of the Virgin Mary, he has truly been made one of us, like to us in all things except sin."[21] We too easily forget that the vast bulk of Christ's life was spent in obscure, mundane, painfully ordinary work, but not any less redemptive for that. In living the fullness of human reality—birth, adolescence, adulthood, death, study, and work—Christ redeems everything. Not just the soul is saved, but everything is sanctified and made capable of sanctifying us, for Christ did all things well (Mark 7:37). Consequently, Christians are to *love* the world, and to love the world with real depth and fullness, and in so doing realize the unity of God's affirmation of created goodness as well as the new creation of Christ. We are to love the world in all its richness and variation, plenitude and effervescence, and our passionate love for the world in its form and furnishings is our sanctification and worship of God.

7. Christian life, and by extension Christian education, is first contemplative, first a training in recognizing and delightfully affirming the goodness, truth, beauty, number, order, and being of creation and creatures:

> For this to happen, we need first of all to *foster*, in ourselves and in others, *a contemplative outlook*. Such an outlook arises from faith in the God of life, who has crated every individual as a 'wonder' (cf. *Ps* 139:14). It is the outlook of those who see life in its deeper meaning, who grasp its utter gratuitousness, its beauty and its invitation to freedom and responsibility. It is the outlook of those who do not presume to take possession of reality but instead accept it as a gift, discovering in all things the reflection of the Creator and seeing in every person his living image.[22]

Such contemplation responds with joy and praise, with love. Love, before it is anything else, is approval "in the literal sense of the word's root: loving someone or something means finding him or it *probus*, the Latin word for 'good'. It is a way of turning to him or it and saying, 'It's good that you exist; it's good that you are in this world.'"[23]

21. Ibid., 8.
22. John Paul II, *Evangelium Vitae*, 83.
23. Pieper, *Faith, Hope, Love*, 163–64.

8. All that is, insofar as it has being, is intelligible or knowable; all that is, insofar as it has its proper perfection, is good and beautiful. Moreover, inasmuch as anything has goodness and being it is self-communicative—it gives itself to be known and delighted in—for "[b]y nature, the good of each thing is its act and perfection. Now, each thing acts in so far as it is in act, and in acting it diffuses being and goodness to other things."[24] All being, in direct proportion to its degree of interior perfection or self-governance—introversion or solitude—is thereby also "'extraverted,' or *towards-others*," or capable of self-donation.[25] Everything gives itself to be known and approved and is, in a certain sense, perfected when known and approved by persons, for the universe is personal, ordered toward person. At the same time, the human person gives themselves to be known and approved in a more perfect manner than the non-personal, but in knowing and delighting in other things, the human gives of their own operation of self-diffusiveness, not only recognizing the perfection of the world but operating in keeping with their own perfection in doing so. That is, in contemplating and approving the world, both the world and the human acts in keeping with finality or teleology. It is good to do, for both ourselves and the world. The *theoretical* or contemplative life is thus the first task, for it is an "*openness to the things that are*," an attitude or "disposition . . . to receive what things have to tell us," and what they have to tell us, more than anything, is the "great, even infinite depth present within them," the divine fecundity "immanent within them."[26] As we passionately love the world, which we do first by attending to and recognizing the world, allowing and enabling its own received generosity to diffuse, we love God.

## Freedom and Work

9. Christian education begins with the theoretical or contemplative disposition for the very same reason that the human person is called to go beyond mere receptivity and engage the world through work, thereby reshaping and developing creation, namely, "operation is the

24. Aquinas, *Summa Contra Gentiles*, I. 37.

25. Clarke, *Person and Being*, 15–16; cf. John Paul II, *Man and Woman He Created Them*, 178–87.

26. Schmitz, *Recovery of Wonder*, 24–47.

ultimate perfection of each thing."[27] The theoretical disposition is a perfective operation, but so too is labor, and the Benedictine maxim of *ora et labora*—pray and work—gives us the educational ideal of "intellectuals with dirt under their fingernails."[28] This because we are created in the image of God:

> Man is made to be in the visible universe an image and likeness of God himself, and he is placed in it in order to subdue the earth. From the beginning therefore he is *called to work. Work is one of the characteristics that distinguish* man from the rest of creatures, whose activity for sustaining their lives cannot be called work. Only man is capable of work, and only man works, at the same time by work occupying his existence on earth. Thus work bears a particular mark of man and of humanity, the mark of a person operating within a community of persons.[29]

All human activity, "whether manual or intellectual," responds to the "mandate received from [the] Creator to subdue the earth. In carrying out this mandate, man, every human being, reflects the very action of the Creator of the universe."[30]

10. While work, manual or intellectual, subdues the earth, good work does not "submit it to torture and in a wracking inquisition extract" answers and benefits out of keeping with the good of creation:[31] "The Creator's directive to humankind means that it is supposed to look after the world as God's creation, and to do so in accordance with the rhythm and logic of creation. . . . the world is to be used for what it is capable of and for what it is called to, but not for what goes against it. . . . "[32] Work is *perfective*, it brings to mature act the latent possibilities of a good creation, including its knowability and possible advance in intelligibility. In a primary sense, the purpose of work is the "subject of work, that is to say the person, *the individual who carries it out*."[33]

27. Aquinas, *Summa Contra Gentiles*, I. 113.

28. Schmitz, *Recovery of Wonder*, 37.

29. John Paul II, *Laborem Exercens*, "Blessing".

30. Ibid., 4.

31. Ratzinger, *In the Beginning*, 35.

32. Ibid., 34.

33. John Paul II, *Laborem Exercens*, 6.

In the "dominating" aspect of work, the human is called to subdue the world because, like God, the human "is a subjective being capable of acting in a planned and rational way, capable of deciding about himself, and with a tendency to self-realization. As *a person, man is therefore the subject of work.*"[34] Work is a form of self-governance or self-rule, an exercise in freedom, and in working the person confirms and perfects themselves as personal. Intellectual work, like all forms of labor, is emancipatory and perfective, it seeks to make us free and does so in an intrinsic and constitutive way, i. e., the labor of education bears the capacity to render liberty without regard to any external benefits or by-products. Consequently, to educate others, to lead others into theory, is an act of spiritual mercy, a basic act of justice requiring no justification other than itself—the work of education is a basic human good.

11. In addition to its subjective dimension, there is *"an objective sense, which finds expression in the various epochs of culture and civilization,"* including the industry, tools, and technology of those cultures and civilizations.[35] Work contributes to a fully articulated vision of development in basic needs such as food, shelter, and health, but also in more advanced goods such as the rule of law and economic systems, and even into the domain of personal, cultural, and religious values.[36] Work and study allows for and secures human development in all these domains in direct and indirect ways, even as intellectual work allows for ongoing reflection on the ethics of human development and the means of seeking it. As a result, Catholic education embraces every domain of human capacity, seeking both to further development as well as judgment about the meaning and morality of that development. Humanities, social sciences, professional training, the pure sciences, applied sciences, all are engaged as (a) contributing to the subjective perfection of the student/teacher/worker, (b) as they contribute to authentic and integral human development, and (c) insofar as the work is in keeping with the worth and primacy of the person in both their individuality and sociality. That is, "on condition that the objective dimension of work does not gain the upper hand over the

34. Ibid.

35. Ibid., 5.

36. Benedict XVI, *Caritas in Veritate*, 25; cf. Lonergan, *Method in Theology*, 27–57 and *Topics in Education*, 26–79.

subjective dimension, depriving man of his dignity and inalienable rights or reducing them," including the rights of the family, networks of subsidiarity and solidarity, and the goods of human culture.[37]

12. While the Church claims her due authority in matters of doctrine and morality, and while she offers her expertise in humanity to the world, the Church claims no special knowledge or prerogative in the various disciplines and domains of human activity. The Church posits no particular philosophy, although, to be sure, human action is caught up in both the subjective dimensions of work and the integral development of its objective implications and so the Church's task of discernment, her labor of reading the signs of the time, is ongoing and speaks to the purposes and tasks of every human enterprise.[38] Still, in conversation with broader implications regarding human well-being, each discipline and activity possesses its own internal coherence and integrity, and by that integrity the discipline is responsible and self-regulated. All that exists possesses its own perfection and form, its own internal depths, rhythm and inner logic; so Catholic education cheerfully recognizes the rightful integrity and autonomy of "earthly affairs," including the arts, sciences, professional programs and so forth. Seeing no need to conform all activity to a pre-established worldview or static system, the Catholic mind is catholic, welcoming each human development and progress, for "by the subjection of all things to man, the name of God would be wonderful in all the earth."[39] There is a genuine autonomy whereby "created things and societies themselves enjoy their own laws and values which must be gradually deciphered, put to use, and regulated by men . . . for by the very circumstance of their having been created, all things are endowed with their own stability, truth, goodness, proper laws, and order."[40] Catholic education, thus, embraces a kind of "Christian secularity,"[41] a rejection of integralism—even the integralism of worldview analysis so popular with some forms of Christian education—as it allows the world to be the world.[42]

37. John Paul II, *Laborem Exercens*, 10 ff; cf. *Compendium of Social Doctrine*, 76–78, 160–63.

38. John Paul II, *Veritatis Splendor*, 29–30; cf. *Guadium et Spes*, 34–36.

39. *Guadium et Spes*, 34.

40. Ibid., 36.

41. Rhonheimer, *The Common Good of Constitutional Democracy*, 307–9.

42. For analysis of the shortcomings of the worldview approach, see Snell and Cone,

13. With respect to modern and contemporary developments and the crisis of meaning and culture often perceived as endemic to our time, many respond with fear, others with unreasonable optimism. Catholic education repeats the words so often expressed by the messengers of God—"Be not afraid." The "profound and rapid changes . . . [t]riggered by the intelligence and creative energies of man" with respect to science, technology, medicine, communication, industry, trade, mores, and political systems have created "spiritual agitation" and "many people are shaken," and yet the demands for dignity, freedom, autonomy, development, and knowledge concomitant with the contemporary situation reveal both the dignity of the human *and* an increased awareness of that autonomous dignity.[43] While many of the ways in which these demands are actualized are counter to the truth, the basic values behind such demands regard "the quest for the values proper to the human spirit."[44] Modernity challenged the Church's self-understanding and claims on many issues, and as modernity works itself out it often seems vulnerable and prone to a variety of troubling vices, including the status of faith and matters of life and morals, even as it succumbs to individualism, disenchantment, instrumentalization of creation and persons, and "soft"-depotism, and yet a powerful moral idea of human freedom undergirds them, a value "conferred by God on man" and "thus exceedingly good."[45]

14. In light of this, Catholic education maintains a commitment to the very best of the old and the new—*nova et vetera*—in a mode of creative fidelity. Steeped in classical culture and thought, Catholicism views the "rapprochement between Biblical faith and Greek philosophical inquiry" as "an event of decisive importance" and, rather than viewing dehellenization as a recovery, considers "the critically purified Greek heritage [as] an integral part" of the development of Christian faith.[46] In particular, faith becomes reasonable, or certainly not unreasonable, and the tradition of theology is thus one of wisdom,

---

*Authentic Cosmopolitanism*, 1–12.

43. *Guadium et Spes*, 4–10; *Dignitatis Humanae*, 1.

44. *Dignitatis Humanae*, 1.

45. *Guadium et Spes*, 11; Taylor, *Ethics of Authenticity*, 1–17.

46. Benedict XVI, *Regensburg Address*.

knowledge, argument, conversation, rather than bald assertion, pure will, or arbitrariness; theology becomes a science, the highest science:

> . . . we can see the profound harmony between what is Greek in the best sense of the word and the biblical understanding of faith in God . . . God acts, σὺν λόγω, with *logos*. *Logos* means both reason and word - a reason which is creative and capable of self-communication, precisely as reason . . . In the beginning was the *logos*, and the *logos* is God, says the Evangelist. The encounter between the Biblical message and Greek thought did not happen by chance. The vision of Saint Paul, who saw the roads to Asia barred and in a dream saw a Macedonian man plead with him: "Come over to Macedonia and help us!" (cf. *Acts* 16:6-10) - this vision can be interpreted as a "distillation" of the intrinsic necessity of a rapprochement between Biblical faith and Greek inquiry.[47]

As a result, Catholic education places high value on the sources, the origins, returning to Scripture, antiquity, the Fathers, and the medieval masters again and again—*ad fontes*—with genuine piety and new questions in the tension of return and renewal, for this pious regard for the old always anticipates vitality—ever ancient, ever new.

15. But the return to the sources is not closed, for our questions change in light of ongoing discoveries in every discipline and field of study, and Catholicism believes not only in the development of doctrine and the ongoing task of the Church but also dynamism of the human spirit and intellect. God, it is believed, can be found in all things, and at all times and places, if we would listen well, and there is an ease— sometimes an overly unguarded ease—of engagement with diverse sources. Most obvious has been the engagement with modern science, economics, political theory, the human and social sciences, and with postmodern critique. Perhaps as evident, and every bit as momentous, is ongoing development of a genuinely catholic pluralism, including the recognition of non-Western and non-European voices. Such has a profoundly destabilizing tendency as older certitudes are expressed differently, contextualized, or even called into question. (Consider the transformation of Jesuit education from the *Ratio Studiorum* to the contemporary Ignatian mode, as just one example.)

47. Ibid.

16. Such instability tends to foster the creation of a solid camp of *traditionalists*, those determined to live and move and have their being in the old, the *vetera*, highlighting the permanent attainments of the tradition in the face of current skepticism or instability. In a similar way, there tends to be formed various camps of *progressives*, sometimes those committed to the promise contained within the *nova* and largely indifferent to the old, and sometimes those rather more hostile to the old, those viewing their task as destructive, as an annihilation of the older ways. For the Catholic mind, the extremes are mistakes, for reason and progress lies not in thoughtless or destructive progress nor in moribund traditionalism but in *tradition*, the ongoing conversation and tension maintaining continuity with the permanent while challenging its understanding. Catholic education embraces its heritage, its rootedness, its placed-ness, even as it welcomes historicity, plurality, difference, freedom, dynamism. As such, Catholic education is humanistic, in that it acknowledges always the importance of originative texts and their ongoing status to the conversation; hermeneutical, in that it recognizes the ongoing nature of conversation and deliberation; critical, in that it challenges itself according to its own inner logic and sources even as it welcomes challenges from other traditions; and developmental, in that it expects to continue in deep continuity with its past even as it changes. All this is to say that it is a tradition with a tradition-constituted rationality which does not grant the supremacy of any alien account but also includes and incorporates the best of other traditions into its own self-understanding and self-articulation.[48] This explains, in part, the relative ease with which Catholicism embraces local piety and ritual (which smacks of syncretism to some detractors), and its lack of panic about modern science, while retaining its placid assurance and composure about theology or morality thought determined or defined (which smacks of dogmatism to some detractors). But reasonable traditions display this kind of elastic permanence, and in this respect Catholicism seems redolent of that Chestertonian maxim that a man thought too skinny by some and too fat by others might be, in fact, just about right.

48. MacIntyre, *Whose Justice? Which Rationality?*, 349–89; *Three Rival Versions*, 127–237.

17. This elastic permanence or creative fidelity also accounts in part for the diversity of Catholic models of education. The Sisters of St. Joseph are not Dominicans or Benedictines or Jesuits or members of the Congregation of the Holy Cross. And yet all, in their own unique way, are authentically Catholic models of education. Reality is large, and good, and there are many ways to contemplate, approve, and work in keeping with that goodness.

## Healing in History

18. The expansive, pluralistic, hopeful, and irenic mode of Catholic education should be understood rightly. Autonomy is valued and expresses a deep truth, but if autonomy "is taken to mean that created things do not depend on God, and that man can use them without any reference to their Creator" then unintelligibility beckons.[49] In a similar way, progress brings with it "a strong temptation," especially if "the order of values is jumbled."[50] Catholic education is hardly naïve (let alone Pelagian) about progress or autonomy or human capacity:

> For a monumental struggle against the powers of darkness pervades the whole history of man. The battle was joined from the very origins of the world and will continue until the last day. Caught in this conflict, man is obliged to wrestle constantly if he is to cling to what is good. Nor can he achieve his own integrity without valiant efforts and the help of God's grace.[51]

In addition to the love of light, there is the love of darkness: "when man looks into his own heart he finds that he is drawn toward what is wrong and sunk in many evils which cannot come from his good creator."[52]

19. The prelapsarian unity and harmony is "destroyed . . . shattered . . . broken," and the world "is virtually inundated with sin."[53] So, too, is the individual as student, teacher, and learner, and in their entire be-

---

49. *Guadium et Spes*, 36.
50. Ibid., 37.
51. Ibid.
52. Ibid., 13.
53. *Catechism of the Catholic Church*, 400–1.

ing, including their intellect. This is not to suggest that human nature is annihilated or somehow not good, for "sin neither adds to nor takes away from human nature," even as the proper functioning of that nature is seriously damaged.[54] Original justice, the grace allowing for the unity, harmony, and complete functioning of the human is lost, and among the wounds of sin is included the wound of ignorance, a failure to know what can and ought to be known; further, the impairment of will includes the failure to even want to know, let alone live rightly in keeping with reason and knowledge.[55] Consequently, a Catholic view of learning and life assumes that persons are damaged and wounded by sin, not in a proper relationship to God, themselves, the world, their intellects, will, or knowledge.

20. It assumes also the reality and efficacy of grace. Of course, the university is not the Church and administers no sacraments and holds no keys of forgiveness. Still, because grace presupposes and perfects nature, grace works in keeping with the structures of human reality, including our subjectivity, sociality, physicality, and so on. Consequently, "all created reality, even the least of it, the most ordinary and prosaic, has a lasting meaning. Taken up into [God's] love, the created order plays a decisive role in the unfolding of the spiritual growth effected by the Spirit of God. . . . Except for the structures of sin, every earthly reality opens itself to the redeeming love of Christ and becomes—precisely as an earthly reality and *according to its own logic*—a path for this love, capable of being sanctified and saturated with the spirit of God."[56] This is possible only because of the work of Christ, of course, but that work confirms the goodness of all things and their mediation of grace, even as they maintain their own nature. Most of us become saints in the ordinary work and details of life, through our work, including the intellectual work of research, teaching, and learning. To be sure, "the sacraments are decisive for enabling the life of grace to grow in us," and the Catholic teacher or student recognizes that intellectual work does not replace them, let alone act as the originator of sanctifying grace, and yet ordinary work and life "becomes cooperation in the work of redemption and unfolds as a way of personal holiness

54. Gilson, *Spirit of Mediaevel Philosophy*, 125.

55. For more on this, see Snell and Cone, *Authentic Cosmopolitanism*, especially 87–130.

56. Rhonheimer, *Changing the World*, 6–8, emphasis added.

and apostolate."[57] For the non-Catholic and non-Christian, even for those not in right relationship with God, intellectual work remains a place of possible encounter with God, for the original goodness of Creation remains buried deep down things, and the *Logos* carried within them is the same *Logos* which redeemed and still redeems all things, and who speaks constantly, always desiring to communicate his goodness, love, and redemption to each and every creature. God is not silent, nor does he speak only to some, but his Word calls out from every being and to every person and can be found in any ordered activity or discipline:

> . . . God creates this universe precisely in order to invite other persons into the relational life of the Trinity. God's purpose or intention of inviting each person . . . is not episodic, occurring periodically in each person's life. God is always acting to bring about this intention . . . at every moment of our existence God is communicating to us who God is, is trying to draw us into an awareness, a consciousness of the reality of who we are in God's sight. Whether we are aware of it or not, at every moment of our existence we are encountering God.[58]

Thus, even the labor and action of study, which carries with it its own possibility of subjective and objective perfection, has as its origin and end contemplation: origin, in that the first task is recognizing the goodness and depth of things; end, in that all things can lead us into a disposition of openness to and love of God.

21. The university, in following out its own logic, becomes an avenue of redemption, without thereby becoming something other than it is or supplanting the Church and sacrament in the economy of salvation. In the *subjective* dimension of intellectual work, the university allows the development of virtue, personal and social collaboration in sanctification, and a working out of holiness and vocation. In acting, we are perfected. With respect to the *objective* dimension of intellectual work, the university's capacity for collaboration, research, discovery, and transmission of knowledge in a wide range of activities provides a uniquely powerful role in supporting integral human development in its full range, from basic necessities to institutional systems to

57. Ibid., 12.
58. Barry, *Finding God in All Things*, 12.

civilizational goods and cultural reflection and production. Like all things, the university's contribution to technology, medicine, agriculture, policy and so on is judged judged by human flourishing human flourishing, including the fundamental principles of social doctrine: the common good, the universal destination of goods, subsidiarity, participation, solidarity, and the values of truth, freedom, and justice.[59] The intellectual and social dynamism of the university allows for contributions to human progress, for the nature of the universe is "friendly" and ordered, meaning that following reason tends to result in cumulative and progressive development:

> . . . this process of new ideas can spread through the whole good of order. You start changing the situation . . . [n]ew ideas will start popping up everywhere. There will result augmented well-being, and it affects each of the aspects of the human good: the flow of particular goods becomes more frequent, more instant, more varied; . . . new types of goods are provided; the society enjoys democracy and more education . . . there is status for all, because everything is running smoothly . . . there are happy personal relations, a development in taste, in aesthetic value and its appreciation, and in ethics, in the autonomy of the subject finally there is more time for people to attend to their own perfection in religion.[60]

Obviously this is an ideal, and reality rarely works this way, but still intelligence and reason tend toward better ideas, better policy, better social relations, a better ethical situation, and so forth, and the university has something to contribute to that end—the university exists in service to others.

22. Because of sin, cumulative progress is not necessary, perhaps not even very likely, and the university and its members suffer from the disorientation of sin even while remaining good. Without sacrificing its own internal logic in any way, the university can benefit from the presence and gift of the Church. First, the theology and social teaching of the Church provides a true account of the nature and destiny of human beings and what is due them given their status as persons. Second, the faithful, having encountered the person of Christ and being renewed by the gift of the theological virtues, have a redemptive role:

59. *Compendium of Social Doctrine*, 71–72.

60. Lonergan, *Topics in Education*, 51.

> . . . The supernatural virtues of faith, hope, and charity . . .
> orientate man to God as he is in himself. Nonetheless, they
> possess a profound social significance. Against the perpetua-
> tion of explosive tensions . . . there is the power of charity. . . .
> Against the economic determinism . . . there is the liberating
> power of hope. . . . Against the dialectic discernible in the . . .
> development-and-decline of civil and cultural communities,
> there is the liberation of human reason through divine faith.[61]

Faith is never reduced to social progress, but it is not irrelevant to
social progress, and while there is no such thing as Christian math or
Catholic physics or Christian economics, nor even, except in the historical sense, a Christian art or Catholic music, those who are made
free by grace to act again as *full humans* do contribute to the redemptive perfection of each. Those who love well, do well.

## Fidelity

23. Some tension may appear between the claims of autonomy and refer-
    ences to theology, social doctrine, and the redemptive nature of faith
    in the university. Of course the entire set of theses is a theology of
    education, but a theology explaining the rightful ground of autonomy
    or secularity of nature, reason, study, and the university. The natural
    remains natural, free—even obligated—to follow its own structures,
    although it is theology which explains this freedom and autonomy
    best without thereby impairing autonomy in any way. Theology serves
    an integrative role, providing unity to the fragmentation endemic to
    the contemporary specialized university by providing an account of
    the origin and destiny of the individual, society, and all of history,
    thereby giving meaning and place to the various disciplines and fields
    of study. A full account always requires a narrative, and while meth-
    odological reductionism provides a bounty relative to the parts, an
    overarching account is needed so that the parts can *mean*, let alone
    that the parts can *mean* with respect to the purpose of life. As the uni-
    versity fragments, and as postmodernism culls the *ersatz* religions of
    pure reason, theology retains an essential task in providing meaning.
    Nothing in the methodology of contemporary discourse disallows
    this, for modern study has succeeded insofar as it has concentrated on

61. Lonergan, *Collection*, 111–12.

efficient and material causality—on *explanations of cause*—whereas theology (and the theologically informed philosophical anthropology to which Catholicism has contributed so much) concerns itself with *understanding* and with final causality. Fundamentalism tends to err in thinking that theology provides causal explanation; it does not, but it does seek to *understand* the meaning of the explanations. Scientism tends to err in thinking that methodological naturalism provides understanding; it does not, but it does explain causes, and ought to do so in keeping with its own autonomous logic.

24. In keeping an eye to *understanding* even as it pursues the ordinary intellectual work of *explanation*, an authentic Catholic education attempts something rather more than its public counterparts, for it offers *paideia*, an account of life, a story of human well-being, of the meaning and purpose of it all and our place and responsibility within the whole. So more is offered—everything is offered—but nothing is lost from the wide and exhilarating range of human accomplishment and excellence. Still, since Catholicism denies the possibility of freedom without truth, its education must at times serve as a sign of contradiction to the commonsense of its age.[62] From time to time, authentic human progress requires dissent, even rebellion, and in her mission of proclaiming the deep amazement and wonder of human persons and the God who made them, authentically Catholic education dissents from anything which degrades the person or the institutions and structures necessary to personal flourishing. Given the Magisterium's authority in matters of faith and morals, Catholic education is called to fidelity to the teaching office *in order to preserve a rightful autonomy and dignity of the person*. All members of Catholic universities, whether Catholic or not, thus have a responsibility to acknowledge the right of the Magisterium to teach on these matters—although with no particular expertise beyond them—and particularly the right to judge the competency of theologians claiming to represent Catholic thought. Even when a Catholic university or its faculty genuinely believes the Church to be in error, they must acknowledge the Church's status as "communal mediator of the faith," and should accept the rights of the Church to exercise that task.[63] In no way does this threaten the intel-

62. John Paul II, *Veritatis Splendor*, 31–32.
63. Marshall, "Theologian's Ecclesial Vocation," para. 23. See also John Paul II, *Ex*

lectual enterprise, for orthodoxy opens a clearing for the intellect and its questions, and while orthodoxy begins with a judgment of what is in fact the case, this judgment demands further questions of *how* this could be true, and so the further questions of wonder emerge as faith seeks understanding—*fides quarens intellectum.*

25. Finally, while the Catholic tradition embraces and instantiates a robust and living tradition of intellectual life, hosting among its members Augustine, Thomas Aquinas, Duns Scotus, Catherine of Sienna, Edith Stein, Copernicus, and Mendel, to name just a few, it has never measured a life "in the magnitude of one's intellectual attainments" but rather in how "one exercised his or her freedom. The Great Commandment is: Thou shall love the Lord thy God with thy whole heart and mind and soul, and thy neighbor as thyself."[64] Catholic education begins and ends in love, in the joyful contemplation of the goodness of all things, especially persons, in the work which perfects this good creation while allowing progress and human development, and in the love of God who creates, sustains, and redeems this good earth.

> The whole concern of doctrine and its teaching must be directed to the love that never ends. Whether something is proposed for belief, for hope or for action, the love of our Lord must always be made accessible, so that anyone can see that all the works of perfect Christian virtue spring from love and have no other objective than to arrive at love.[65]

The glory of God is man fully alive, but persons are most alive when they love, and education exists to lead us to such a life.

# Bibliography

Aquinas, Thomas. *Summa Contra Gentiles.* Sourced from Public Domain.

Barry, William A. *Finding God in All Things: A Companion to the Spiritual Exercises of St. Ignatius.* Naples, FL: Ave Maria Press, 2009

Benedict XVI. *The Regensburg Lecture.* Edited with introduction by James V. Schall, SJ. South Bend: St. Augustine Press, 2007.

*Catechism of the Catholic Church.* United States Conference of Catholic Bishops, 2005.

Clarke, W. Norris. *Person and Being.* Milwaukee: Marquette University Press, 1993.

*Corde Ecclesiae.*

64. Monan, in Snell and Cone, *Authentic Cosmopolitanism*, 3.

65. *Catechism of the Catholic Church*, 25.

*Compendium of Social Doctrine.* United States Conference of Catholic Bishops, 2005.

The following Encyclicals of the Catholic Church can be found at
http://www.papalencyclicals.net:

*Dei Verbum*

*Evangelium Vitae,*

*Redemptor Hominis*

*Laborem Exercens,*

*Caritas in Veritate*

*Guadium et Spes*

*Dignitatis Humanae*

Gilson, Etienne. *Spirit of Mediaeval Philosophy.* Translated by Cécile Gilson. New York: Random House, 1952.

John Paul II. *Man and Woman He Created Them. A Theology of the Body.* Translated by Michael Waldstein. Boston: Pauline Books and Media, 2006.

Lonergan, Bernard. *Method in Theology.* Toronto: University of Toronto Press, 1990.

———. *Topics in Education.* Toronto: University of Toronto Press, 1988.

MacIntyre, Alasdair. *Three Rival Versions.* South Bend: University of Notre Dame Press, 1991.

———. *Whose Justice? Which Rationality?* South Bend: University of Notre Dame Press, 1989.

Marshall, Bruce D. "The Theologian's Ecclesial Vocation," http://www.firstthings.com/article/2013/10 /the-theologians-ecclesial-vocation

Monan, J. Donald S. J. Quoted in R. J. Snell and Steven D. Cone, *Authentic Cosmopolitanism.* Eugene: Pickwick, 2013.

Pieper, Josef. *Faith, Hope, Love.* Translated by George and Clara Winston. New York: Random House, 1963.

Ratzinger, Joseph Cardinal. *In the Beginning . . . : A Catholic Understanding of the Story of Creation and the Fall.* Translated by Boniface Ramsey. Grand Rapids: Eerdmans, 1995.

Rhonheimer, Martin. *The Common Good of Constitutional Democracy: Essays in Political Philosophy and on Catholic Social Teaching.* Translated by William F. Murphy. Washington, DC: Catholic University Press, 2012

Schmitz, Kenneth L. *Recovery of Wonder: The New Freedom and The Asceticism Of Power.* Montreal: McGill University Press, 2005

Snell, R. J., and Steven D. Cone. *Authentic Cosmopolitanism.* Eugene: Pickwick, 2013.

Taylor, Charles. *Ethics of Authenticity.* Cambridge: Harvard University Press, 1992.

# CHAPTER THREE

# A Lutheran View of Life and Learning:
# Paradox as Paradigm

*Korey D. Maas*

DESPITE INAUGURATING THE UNQUESTIONABLY world-changing Reformation of the sixteenth century, and remaining even in the twenty-first century the world's second largest Protestant tradition, Lutherans are not often perceived—when they are perceived at all—as particularly substantive contributors to modern public life and thought. Indeed, in their public presence American Lutherans especially have been, as the historian Mark Noll once observed, "remarkably unremarkable." It is worth quickly noting, however, that this remark—made by a non-Lutheran—was not at all meant dismissively; to the contrary, it might best be understood as something of a lament, for Noll goes on to praise "the penetrating vision of Luther, the scholarly aplomb of Melanchthon, the irenic efficiency of the Concord formulators, the surging brilliance of Bach, the passionate wisdom of Kierkegaard, [and] the heroic integrity of Bonhoeffer," concluding that, avoiding possible mis-steps, "the resources that Lutherans offer to Americans, especially other Protestants, would be of incalculable benefit."[1] Nor is Noll alone in offering such an assessment; other non-Lutherans have noted the same, remarking especially favorably on "the rich resources for sustaining the life of the mind that reside in the Lutheran heritage."[2]

It is by means of this "heritage" that the following pages will provide a summary sketch of a distinctively Lutheran view of life and learning. Thus,

---

1. Noll, "The Lutheran Difference," 31, 33, and 37.

2. Hughes, *The Vocation of the Christian Scholar*, 62.

while the continuing viability and relevance of this view will, it is hoped, become evident, what follows will of necessity give particular attention to the sixteenth century, where Lutheranism's distinctive features first become evident. Some warrant for giving special attention to the sixteenth century might also be found in a number of striking similarities between that age and our own—the most frequently discussed, perhaps especially in the context of educational concerns, being the revolutions in communications technology distinctive of each era. Not unrelated, but more immediately relevant to the topic at hand, however, is Lewis Spitz's observation than "at no other time in the history of the world, except perhaps our own, has so much attention been paid to educational theory and reform as in the age of the Renaissance and Reformation."[3] And much of this attention was fueled by concerns that will sound neither foreign nor antiquated.

So, for example, with the substitution of only a couple words, many contemporary educators will have heard precisely what Martin Luther complained of hearing so regularly in his day: "If my son learns enough to earn a penny, he is learned enough." Those attracted to the life of academe as one lived in pursuit of the true, the good, and the beautiful, will similarly lament with Luther that "nobody wants to rear children for anything else than the knowledge and ability to make a living."[4] And yet, given the state of many universities, one will also, like Luther, sympathize with those who are skeptical about the value of four or more years—and great sums of money—spent in their environs. So, for instance, asking the same question raised by many who have read Tom Wolfe's still relatively recent—and depressingly accurate—novel of collegiate life, *I Am Charlotte Simmons*, Luther could write, "what have [people] been learning till now in the universities . . . except to become asses, blockheads, and numbskulls, . . . to say nothing of the scandalous and immoral life there in which many a fine young [person] was shamefully corrupted"?[5]

Though of course primarily known for his critique of much late medieval theology, such representative quotations reveal that Luther was also regularly critical of much contemporary thought in and about the university. Yet he was never merely a critic; in the realms of both theology and

3. Spitz, "Luther and Humanism," 88.

4. Plass, ed., *What Luther Says*, no. 1331. In the same passage Luther refers to those holding such an attitude as "the most noxious and harmful folk on earth."

5. Luther, *To the Councilmen of All Cities in Germany*, in *Luther's Works*, 45:351–52. Shortly thereafter, on the same page, he refers more pointedly to contemporary schools as "asses' stalls and devil's training centers."

education he and his colleagues actively and continually sought reform and renewal, with the result that it might be worth speaking of *two* reformations emanating from sixteenth-century Wittenberg. Or, it might be worth speaking of two reformations if the theological and educational could be separated. But James Kittleson is certainly correct in suggesting that in fact they cannot be, that, instead, "the Reformation itself may be rightly understood as a massive educational undertaking."[6]

Indeed, while it remains common to speak of the "reformation" with reference to the theological revisions of the sixteenth-century, it has often been noted that Luther's own appeals to reform are first and frequently made with reference to curricular revision, as for instance, in his judgment that "there is no work more worthy of pope or emperor than a thorough reform of the universities. And on the other hand, nothing could be more devilish or disastrous than unreformed universities."[7] Similarly, though textbook narratives will date the origins of the German reformation to the posting of Luther's "Ninety-Five Theses" against indulgences in October of 1517, it has often been noted that his earlier theses of the same year were, though often overlooked, far more radical in their content. These ninety-seven theses, not against indulgences but against scholastic theology, were an explicit assault on the curriculum of the medieval university,[8] which became part of the impetus for the dramatic reorientation of Wittenberg's own curriculum, beginning in earnest the following year with the arrival of the young humanist scholar—and later author of Lutheranism's primary confessional document—Philip Melanchthon.

The intimate relationship between the theological and the pedagogical which existed in the minds of Luther, Melanchthon, and their colleagues is more than borne out by their educational activities and emphases, and was amply evident to their contemporaries. Not only was Melanchthon's advice constantly sought by universities seeking to reform themselves along the lines of Wittenberg, but he would also be instrumental in the founding of several new universities. The still-famous German *Gymnasia* serving as university prep-schools were one of Melanchthon's creations, and in the decade of the 1520s alone he was invited by more than fifty cities to assist them in establishing their own schools.[9] It is hardly surprising in this light

6. Kittleson, "Luther the Educational Reformer," in *Luther and Learning*, 95.

7. Luther, *To the Christian Nobility of the German Nation*, AE 44:202.

8. Luther, *Disputation Against Scholastic Theology* (1517), AE 31:3–16.

9. Keen, "Introduction," in *A Melanchthon Reader*, 9.

that he would come to be hailed as the *Praeceptor Germaniae*, or teacher of all Germany. This intense Lutheran concern for education, though, would not be confined to Germany, or the sixteenth century. So, for instance, in nineteenth-century America a new Lutheran college was founded, on average, every three years;[10] and even today the relatively small denomination of the Lutheran Church—Missouri Synod oversees the largest Protestant school system in the United States.

Such anecdotal evidence is rattled off not simply for the sake of Lutheran cheerleading,[11] but because it is the sheer scope and intensity of Lutheran interest in education that compels one to ask: Why? The first generation of Lutheran reformers, especially, had more than enough on their hands: drafting doctrinal confessions and church ordinances, engaging in theological controversies with Rome as well as fellow Protestants, and fretting about armed invasion by the emperor, to name just a few. Why take up at the same time the daunting tasks of revising university curricula, founding new universities, reconstituting Latin and vernacular primary schools, and creating an entirely new *Gymnasium* system?

Happily, the reformers were entirely and consistently clear about their reasons for so highly valuing sound education. The first of these, making most explicit the connection between the pedagogical and the theological, is nicely encapsulated in Luther's remark that "God has preserved the church through schools."[12] But, just as often, Luther and his colleagues offer a second explanation for the urgency evident in their activities, and the reference here is not to the church, but to the city, or society more generally. "A city's best and greatest welfare, safety, and strength," Luther remarked, "consists . . . in its having many able, learned, wise, honorable, and cultivated citizens." Indeed, so emphatic was he on the necessity of study also

10. See Noland, "The Lutheran Mind and Its University," *Logia* 17, 45, and Solberg, *Lutheran Higher Education*, 351-2.

11. Indeed, especially with regard to Lutheran education in America, it has rightly been noted that the "most serious critique one could level" is that "it has failed to fulfill the challenges implicit in its own theology." Solberg, "What Can the Lutheran Tradition Contribute to Christian Higher Education?" in *Models for Christian Higher Education*, 80. Nor have people failed to level this critique. Speaking of the colleges and universities of the Lutheran Church—Missouri Synod, Burtchaell, *The Dying of the Light*, writes of their finding it "exceedingly difficult . . . to attain or even aspire to a level of academic accomplishment that would make them attractive on intellectual grounds" (p. 520). He similarly notes that, "academically, no college in the system has had the wherewithal to achieve distinction" (p. 528).

12. Luther, *Table Talk*, AE 54:452.

for "the knowledge and understanding of what to seek and what to avoid in this *outward life*," that he could assert, with perhaps only some hyperbole, that even if

> There were no souls, and there were no need at all of schools and languages for the sake of the Scriptures and of God, this one consideration alone would be sufficient to justify the establishment everywhere of the very best schools . . . namely, that in order to maintain its *temporal estate outwardly* the world must have good and capable men and women.[13]

This point was consistently pressed with some zeal because the Wittenberg reformers were well aware of a pious yet naïve anti-intellectualism which sometimes arose from certain misunderstandings of their theological emphases on grace alone, faith alone, and Scripture alone. "[Y]ou say," Luther quoted some of his contemporaries, "suppose we do have to have schools, what is the use of teaching Latin, Greek, and Hebrew, and the other liberal arts? We could just as well use German for teaching the Bible and God's Word, which is enough for our salvation." After some berating of this opinion as the most certain way to ensure that "we Germans must always be and remain brutes and stupid beasts," Luther defends study of even the "secular" disciplines by insisting that these "can do us no harm, but are actually a greater ornament, profit, glory, and benefit, *both* for the understanding of Holy Scripture *and* the conduct of temporal government."[14] It is precisely this both/and emphasis which is the reformers' most characteristic justification for their educational activities—and, as will become evident, the characteristic paradigm not only for a Lutheran view of learning, but of life itself.

But what sort of education, exactly, did the Lutheran reformers believe best promoted the flourishing of *both* the city of God *and* the city of man? The most concise answer to this question is Luther's own advice to parents: "You parents cannot prepare a more dependable treasure for your children than an education in the liberal arts."[15] This was advice he also gave to

13. Luther, *To the Councilmen*, AE 45:356, 369, and 368 (emphases added); see also 367. Indeed, Luther can even suggest that the most promising students ought to be steered toward service in the temporal estate. See Martin Luther, *A Sermon on Keeping Children in School*, AE 46:241–42.

14. Luther, *To the Councilmen*, AE 45:357–58. See also Luther's and Melanchthon's *Instructions for the Visitors of Parish Pastors in Electoral Saxony*, AE 40:314, which similarly note the purpose of education being "competent service both in church and state."

15. Plass, *What Luther Says*, no. 1319.

himself, even before having children, remarking that, should he be a father, he would encourage his children to study "not only languages and history, but also singing and music, together with the whole of mathematics," not least, he continued, because the ancient Greeks who had so developed these arts, despite their paganism, "grew up to be people of wondrous ability, subsequently *fit for everything*."[16] So, "I beg you also to urge your young people," he would write, "to study poetry and rhetoric diligently."[17] And science, too, since "[w]e are at the dawn of a new era, for we are beginning to recover the knowledge of the external world."[18]

In short, the best education, according to the Lutheran reformers, is a liberal education in "whatever is noble, whatever is right, whatever is pure, whatever is lovely, whatever is admirable."[19] And this is so, especially in the university, because, as John Henry Cardinal Newman would similarly emphasize in the nineteenth century, a university "by its very name professes to teach universal knowledge."[20] Thus, while Melanchthon, in his inaugural address to the students of Wittenberg could exhort them to "dare to know,"[21] Luther himself would further sharpen this by asking, "How dare you not know what can be known"?[22]

It is worth noting at this point, however, that in contrast to some contemporary Christian perspectives on education, there is in Luther and his colleagues a notable absence of any attempt to "baptize" the liberal arts or the disciplines therein. To be sure, as Newman also would, the Lutheran reformers certainly understood that "there are no natural or real limits" between the branches of knowledge,[23] that they are instead interrelated and, therefore, as Luther noted, each is "of use to the other."[24] This is quite clear also in his regular remarks concerning the individual disciplines. "I myself am convinced," he wrote, "that without the knowledge of the literary

---

16. Luther, *To the Councilmen*, AE 45:369 and 370 (emphasis added).

17. Luther, "Letter to Eobanus Hessus," AE 49:34.

18. Quoted in Spitz, *The Renaissance and Reformation Movements*, 2:582.

19. Philippians 4:8 (NIV).

20. Cardinal Newman, *The Idea of a University*, 61.

21. Melanchthon, "On Correcting the Studies of Youth," in *A Melanchthon Reader*, 56.

22. Quoted in Benne, "A Lutheran View of Christian Humanism," in *Christ and Culture in Dialogue*, 320.

23. Newman, *The Idea of a University*, 82.

24. Luther, *Lectures on Genesis*, AE 1:48.

studies, pure theology can by no means exist." In the same vein he further expressed his wish that "there would be a tremendous number of poets and orators, since I realize that through these studies, as through nothing else, people are wonderfully equipped for grasping the sacred truths."[25] And again, "Whoever is to teach others, especially out of Holy Scriptures, and rightly to understand this book, must first have observed and learned to know the world."[26]

But note in such exclamations the typical direction of this relationship between theology and the other arts. Theology is not made the "handmaiden" of science or rhetoric or literature, to serve the creation of some uniquely Christian instantiation of each; rather, in agreement with their medieval predecessors the Lutheran fathers regarded even the "secular" disciplines as handmaids to theology. And yet, these disciplines are not *only* handmaids to theology, and their dignity does not arise merely from their service to theology, but inheres in the disciplines themselves. Thus, in the formulation of Robert Benne, Lutheranism "bestowed tentative autonomy on 'worldly' ways of knowing,"[27] and in Luther's own formulation, "no science should stand in the way of another science, but each should continue to have its own mode of procedure and its own terms."[28] Here again we see the characteristically Lutheran both/and emphases; *both* the sacred *and* the secular sciences are to be esteemed as good in themselves.[29]

Thus far, then, the following appears clear. From the very first, Lutheranism has embodied an extremely high regard for and engagement with educational endeavors. Motivating this has been the firm belief in its necessity for the good of both church and society. The sort of education best suited both to the preservation of sound theology and to the flourishing of human communities is that "most dependable treasure," the liberal education which trains one not for a particular skill or occupation, but renders one "fit for everything." Further, an education fitting one for everything cannot place the "secular" out of bounds. But neither, according

25. Luther, "Letter to Eobanus Hessus," AE 49:34. See also n12 on the same page, which, on the basis of context, glosses Luther's use of the term *literae* ("literary" above), as *bonae literae*, the common term for "humanistic" studies.

26. Quoted in Painter, *Luther on Education*, 148.

27. Benne, "A Lutheran View of Christian Humanism," 320.

28. Luther, *Lectures on Genesis*, AE 1:47.

29. It is this "justification of worldly activity" that sociologist Max Weber famously called "one of the most important results of the Reformation, especially of Luther's part in it." Weber, *The Protestant Ethic and the Spirit of Capitalism*, 81.

to a Lutheran view, will it attempt to collapse the sacred and the secular into a single undistinguished category; the inherent worth of each will be recognized and affirmed.

If this is in any sense an accurate—though certainly by no means complete—sketch of a Lutheran view of learning, questions must now be asked about the broader view of life which informs and is informed by it. Questions must be asked, though it must be admitted at the outset that many Lutherans (the present author included) are made somewhat uncomfortable by them. To speak of a "view of life" sounds very much like speaking of a "worldview," a manner of speaking not historically at home in Lutheranism.[30] For some, antipathy to the concept derives from the suspicion that "worldview" thinking very easily becomes "ideological" thinking, which fails fully to recognize just how darkly we now see through the glass,[31] and which often reveals an unhelpful tendency to ignore, suppress, or distort evidence which might unsettle tidily constructed systems. For others, though, the discomfort comes not from the concept of worldview in itself, but from any claim that there might be a distinctly Lutheran worldview. The fear here is that such a claim betrays an unwarranted sectarianism, because to the extent that Lutherans have a comprehensive and cohesive "philosophy" or "worldview," it is simply that of the universal, small-c-catholic, church.[32]

With this caveat, however, it certainly is possible to speak of some emphases within the Lutheran tradition and its theology which are more or less distinctive, and which have tended to shape Lutheran approaches to both life and learning. The most succinct entrée into these emphases is perhaps the introduction to that work which Luther himself described as presenting "the whole of Christian life in brief form,"[33] his 1520 treatise on

30. Especially revealing in this regard is Naugle's *Worldview: The History of a Concept*, which, while noting that the term "worldview" (*Weltanschauung*) originates and spreads rapidly in Germany, and then is quickly taken up in Scandinavia—both traditionally Lutheran strongholds—the only Lutheran to receive attention for embracing the concept (or, in fact, a variant of it) is Søren Kierkegaard (see pp. 73-82). Indeed, while his survey of the major Christian traditions examines Roman Catholicism, Eastern Orthodoxy, and Protestant Evangelicalism, Naugle makes clear that this last community draws its "worldview tradition" not from Wittenberg and the Lutheran reformers, but from "the theological wellsprings of the reformer from Geneva, John Calvin" (p. 5).

31. See 1 Corinthians 13:12.

32. See, e.g., Meilaender, "The Catholic I Am," 27-30.

33. Luther, *An Open Letter to Pope Leo X*, prefaced to *The Freedom of a Christian*, AE 31:343.

*The Freedom of a Christian.* Here he famously sets forth as his subject matter the ostensibly contradictory theses: "A Christian is a perfectly free lord of all, subject to none. A Christian is a perfectly dutiful servant of all, subject to all."[34] These two sentences perhaps best illustrate that to which this essay's subtitle refers in speaking of paradox as paradigmatic for the Lutheran mind. To be sure, the acknowledgment and even embrace of paradox is not unique to Lutheran Christianity. Blaise Pascal, for instance, famously highlights in his *Pensées* how "paradoxical" man is himself: "Judge of all things, feeble earthworm, repository of truth, sink of doubt and error, the glory and refuse of the universe," whose very "greatness comes from knowing he is wretched."[35] Just as famously, to note only one further example, the eventual Catholic convert G. K. Chesterton devotes a chapter of his classic *Orthodoxy* to "The Paradoxes of Christianity," in which he emphasizes the same.

Moreover, no Christian who, as a Christian, confesses with the creeds that God is three-yet-one, and that the incarnate Christ is fully human and yet fully divine, can escape entanglement with the inherent paradoxes at the very center of the faith. And yet it remains true that Lutheran theology, in light of these shared confessions, has perhaps more than others treated paradox as in some sense paradigmatic. So, for example, Lutherans especially emphasize the Christian's status as *simul justus et peccator*, simultaneously a saint and a sinner. With regard to the sacrament of the altar, as with the doctrine of the incarnation, it is affirmed that the finite can indeed contain the infinite, that Christ with his body and blood are truly present under the mundane forms of bread and wine. Perhaps most importantly for grasping a Lutheran view of life and learning, however, is an understanding of the intertwined paradoxes of God's two words of law and gospel, God's two kingdoms, and the Christian's two kinds of righteousness.

These categories, their import, and their implications will be fleshed out briefly below; but, again, one or two caveats are worth highlighting at the outset. The first is simply that, through the twentieth century, the understanding of Lutheranism's paradoxical nature has been very much informed—and often misinformed—by H. Richard Niebuhr's seminal work, *Christ and Culture.* There he treats Luther's thought—and, it must be noted, that of St. Paul—under the category of "Christ and Culture in Paradox."[36] And while Niebuhr's familiar terminology is here appropriated, the case

34. Luther, *The Freedom of a Christian*, AE 31:344.
35. Pascal, *Pensées*, §131 and §114.
36. Niebuhr, *Christ and Culture*, 149–89.

can be made that many of the emphases which inform it are not, strictly speaking, paradoxical at all. Just as there is no real or apparent contradiction in a father both disciplining as well as doting on his child, neither is there in God speaking to his own children in the two different voices of his law and his gospel,[37] or in the Christian living simultaneously in view of two different ends, the temporal and the eternal. The import of this is especially key in light of Niebuhr's association of paradox with "dualism," sometimes read as a radical separation between, for example, the secular and the sacred, or the realms of creation and redemption. Properly understood, however, the Lutheran paradigm makes distinctions rather than positing strict dichotomies.[38]

Properly understanding these both/and emphases further allows one to avoid any notion of Lutheranism's fetishizing paradox for the sake of paradox, or, as some would charge, reveling in irrationality. Evidence in support of such a charge is, admittedly, not difficult to locate; it is easy enough to cull from the writings of Luther himself potentially embarrassing attacks on reason as, for example, "the devil's greatest whore."[39] And yet Luther's often-criticized hostility to reason must also be viewed in light of his characteristically two-dimensional perspective, because if Luther and his colleagues were indeed as hostile to rationality as is sometimes believed, it would be terribly difficult to account for the inordinate amount of energy they expended in educational endeavors. But explaining this fact is not at all difficult, as the reformers' animus was aimed not at human reason *per se*, but at reason which does not know its proper place or use, which attempts to become an all-encompassing rationalism, and which seeks to rationalize even divine revelation.[40]

Outside of God's revealed mysteries—and most centrally the mystery of salvation itself—Luther is not only happy to let reason reign, but in some respects adamant that it must, as when he insists that "God made the secular government subordinate and subject to reason" and that "[f]or this reason nothing is taught in the Gospel about how it is to be maintained

37. See Kolb, "Niebuhr's 'Christ and Culture in Paradox' Revisited" in Menuge, *Christ and Culture*, 113–14.

38. For brief commentary on this point, see Braaten, "Foreword," in Menuge, *Christ and Culture*, 7-13. It must also be noted that Niebuhr himself is quite clear that "Luther does not, however, divide what he distinguishes." Niebuhr, *Christ and Culture*, 172.

39. Luther, "Sermon for the Second Sunday after Epiphany," in *Werke* 51:126.

40. On this point, see especially Gerrish, *Grace and Reason*.

and regulated."[41] Thus in his shorter *Catechism*, the text which more than any other penned by the reformers has shaped and continues to shape the Lutheran mind and ethos, Luther can confess, on the one hand, that "by my own understanding or strength I cannot believe in Jesus Christ my LORD or come to him," and, on the other, that God himself "has given me and still preserves" my "reason and all mental faculties."[42] The clear implication is that reason, as a good gift of God, dare not be despised—but also dare not be used toward ends improper to it.

This reference to Luther's *Small Catechism* and its two-fold manner of speaking about the good gift of reason, but also its limitations, allows a return, then, to the intertwined paradoxes of God's two words, God's two kingdoms, and the Christian's two kinds of righteousness. Classical Lutheran thought, especially its social thought, is predicated upon a fundamental distinction between what are often referred to as God's two kingdoms, or two realms.[43] Again, this is merely a distinction, and no unbridgeable chasm can be imagined between them, for not only is God himself the King who rules in each kingdom, but so also the Christian lives simultaneously as a citizen in each. But within each realm, the Lutheran holds, God operates and the Christian is oriented toward distinct and different ends. In what is often referred to as the "right-hand" realm, God acts to effect the ultimate and eternal good of man's salvation, while in the "left-hand" realm he acts to establish those penultimate temporal goods which restrain human wickedness and secure human flourishing. As the ends toward which God operates in each realm are distinct, so too are the means through which he operates: in the right-hand kingdom by means of the gospel, communicated in word and sacrament, and received by faith; and in the left-hand kingdom through instruments such as reason and law, and institutions such as families and governments—and universities.

This concept of the two kingdoms fundamentally informs a Lutheran view of learning because, to the extent that Luther and Lutheranism might be said to have anything like a "philosophy" of education, it grows directly out of this distinction, and the existence of the university *qua* university

41. Luther, *Commentary on Psalm 101*, AE 13:198.

42. Luther, *The Small Catechism*, in *The Book of Concord*, 355 and 354.

43. For the classic analysis of Luther's development of these categories, see Wingren, *Luther on Vocation*; see also Wright, *Martin Luther's Understanding of God's Two Kingdoms*.

is placed firmly in the left-hand realm.[44] This is not at all to deny that the university—and any instrument or institution situated in the left-hand kingdom—might also at the same time serve the ultimate ends of the right-hand kingdom. So, for example, in the left-hand realm even an officially secular political regime might, on the basis of *reason*, enshrine in *law* the protection of religious liberty and free speech, thereby safeguarding the public proclamation of the gospel by which eternal salvation is effected and God's right-hand realm populated. More obviously, though, even while a Christian university remains in its essence a university, and not a church, it will certainly provide for the proclamation and explication of the gospel not only in venues such as the college chapel and the theology classroom, but will also encourage the same in less formal social activities and even, where and when appropriate, in the teaching of ostensibly "secular" disciplines.

In speaking of the gospel's proclamation, though, it is important to grasp the precise nature of this distinction between the two kingdoms and the concomitant distinction between God's law and gospel. Much twentieth-century thought has obscured the true nature of these distinctions by, for instance, speaking of God's two realms simply as "the church" and "the state." As already indicated, however, the left-hand kingdom encompasses far more than the state. Equally important to note, though, is that the right-hand realm encompasses far less than "the church," far less even than "theology" in general. The color one paints the bathrooms at First Lutheran may have to do with the church, but it has nothing obvious to do with the gospel, with the forgiveness of sins won by Christ's death and resurrection and imparted to sinners by means of word and sacrament. And it is the gospel, in this very narrow sense, which is operative in the right-hand kingdom. Similarly, then, an excurses on Intelligent Design in the biology lab, a history course's dealing with the faith of the American founders, or the ethics professor's positing that natural law can only be sufficiently grounded in the nature and will of a divine lawgiver may entail some engagement with theology; but where there is no mention of God on a cross for the sinner's forgiveness, there is no proclamation of the gospel *per se*; one is dealing yet in left-hand affairs.

But, the Lutheran will insist, one need not apologize for this, precisely because this left-hand realm in which the university resides is also

44. Solberg similarly notes that "Luther's philosophy of education grew directly out of his concept of the two kingdoms. He placed education squarely within the 'orders of creation' or God's 'secular realm.'" Solberg, "What Can the Lutheran Tradition Contribute?" 76.

God's realm. What is more, not only does one need not apologize for seriously engaging the temporal concerns of this realm, and even doing so without explicit reference to that which is unique to Christianity (the gospel), but so doing may also serve to curb some of the potentially negative consequences of the two-kingdoms paradigm highlighted by Niebuhr and others. These especially include the tendencies toward antinomianism and quietism.[45] That is, according to some dualistic readings of Lutheran paradox, so strong is the temptation to emphasize the ultimate good of the gospel, and the spiritual freedom which faith in the gospel engenders in the right-hand realm, that the left-hand goods of law and reason are slighted or even rejected; the duties and obligations of the left-hand realm are thus abandoned to those who have no dwelling in the right hand kingdom of grace. The Christian is tempted to make of simple distinctions firm and non-overlapping divisions, to say, for example, "My status before God as a forgiven sinner is entirely unmerited and unearned by my good works; therefore there is no need of involving myself in those works which serve the good of civil society."

However real this temptation may be—and certain episodes in Lutheran history suggest that it is real indeed—it betrays what is either a misunderstanding of, or a rejection of, the very substance of the Lutheran paradigm. The substance of the paradox is that the Christian cannot choose to hear only one of God's words, and cannot choose to live in only one of God's kingdoms. The good news (and good-ness) of the gospel does not negate the inherent goodness and necessity of the law, in either its civil or theological expressions; and by way of corollary, the good of the creed's second-article confession of God's gracious redemption does not negate the creed's first-article confession of God's good creation. By virtue of the fact that it is the same Lord who himself situates us in both of his kingdoms, bringing us into life in this left-hand realm of creation, as well as baptizing us into the new life of salvation, the Christian is given the burden—a blessed burden to be sure, but a burden nonetheless—of living faithfully with the tensions of his or her status both *coram deo*, before and in relation to God, and *coram hominibus*, before and in relation to our fellow men.

The Christian's two-fold status in God's two kingdoms thus becomes the basis for the Lutheran's characteristic speaking of two kinds of

---

45. Or what Niebuhr, *Christ and Culture*, 187, refers to as antinomianism and "cultural conservatism." See also, e.g., Menuge, "Niebuhr's *Christ and Culture* Reexamined," in *Christ and Culture in Dialogue*, 42, 46, and 48.

righteousness. In the right-hand kingdom, the Christian's righteousness is the imputed righteousness of Christ himself, received by a faith which is itself a gift of God.[46] It is the righteousness which comes by the gospel and, *coram deo*, it is the "one thing necessary"[47]—indeed, the one thing allowed. *Coram hominibus*, however, the Christian's righteousness is inherent rather than imputed; it is a righteousness defined not by the gospel but by the law; and it is a righteousness necessary not for one's own sake but for the sake of one's neighbor. This is the sum and substance of the ostensibly contradictory theses previously quoted from Luther's treatise on Christian liberty: "A Christian is a perfectly free lord of all, subject to none. A Christian is a perfectly dutiful servant of all, subject to all." That is to say, before and in relation to God, the Christian is perfectly free because God's free gift of salvation requires no work one can offer. Before and in relation to others, however, the Christian remains a dutiful servant whose good works are indeed necessary—not for his own benefit, and certainly not for the benefit of God, but for the sake of others. As Luther concluded, "a Christian lives not in himself, but in Christ and in his neighbor. Otherwise he is not a Christian. He lives in Christ [freely] through faith, in his neighbor [dutifully] through love."[48]

Finally, then, this notion of dutiful service requires an examination of one further distinctive that especially informs a Lutheran view of both life and learning. Those having had the pleasure of reading Cicero may recall the title of one of his more famous works. Usually translated "On Duties," *De Officiis* might also come into English as "On Offices." Suggestive here is that one's *duties* or obligations are associated with and defined by one's *office*, one's calling, or, as Lutherans typically say, one's vocation. That term vocation, though, has a complicated history, morphing from a general connotation in antiquity of any office or station in life; to the medieval reservation of the term for an ecclesiastical office or calling; then to a broadening again in the sixteenth century, especially in Lutheran circles, to any legitimate calling, sacred or secular; and finally being reduced yet again in modernity to a synonym for occupation or paid employment.[49]

---

46. See Ephesians 2:8.

47. Luke 10:42 (New International Version).

48. Luther, *The Freedom of a Christian*, AE 31:371.

49. See Gengenbach, "The Secularization of Vocation and the Worship of Work," *The Cresset* 51:2, 5–13.

Especially in light of its recent and narrow occupational connotations, the term vocation is often treated as anathema in discussions of the college or university, not least those defining themselves as liberal arts institutions. And so there is some potential for confusion when Lutherans consistently and continually emphasize the significance of vocation, using the term in that sense inherited from the sixteenth-century reformers. According to this sense, any legitimate occupation certainly is a vocation; but not all vocations are occupations. Instead, any legitimate calling, standing, station, or office in life is to be understood as a vocation: employee, employer, citizen, sovereign, teacher, student, parent, child, husband, wife. Reflecting something like the emphasis found in Cicero's title, the Lutheran notion recognizes that certain duties inhere in these offices or vocations. But also reflecting a medieval emphasis, Lutherans confess that one does not simply choose one's vocations. Instead, a vocation is a divine calling; one is called into it by God himself. And one is placed by God in vocations precisely so that in his providence God himself might work through these offices, and the fulfillment of their duties, to bestow his blessings on his creatures.

It is sometimes suggested that one of the distinctive marks of the Lutheran mind is its emphatic confession of God's working in both of his kingdoms through mundane secondary causes.[50] This is perhaps most clearly evident in the right-hand realm, where Lutherans are adamant that God's forgiveness of sins is really and truly imparted by means of words and water, bread and wine. But it is no less the case in the left-hand realm, where God effects temporal blessings through such worldly vocational activities as the citizen's casting a vote, the truck-driver's delivering groceries, or the mother's changing of a diaper. "In the exercise of his vocation," Gustav Wingren summarizes Luther, "man becomes a mask for God."[51] That is, God's own good works are hidden behind those performed by fallible human beings simply carrying out the duties of their various offices. "God gives all good gifts," Luther remarks; but "you must work and thus give God good cause and a mask."[52]

The import of this Lutheran view of life for a Lutheran view of learning is, in one respect, quite simple. If it is through the activities relevant to and inhering in one's vocation that God himself "gives all good gifts," then it is incumbent upon one not to get in God's way by negligence or

50. Noland, "The Lutheran Mind and Its University," 49.

51. Wingren, *Luther on Vocation*, 180.

52. Luther, *Commentary on Psalm 147*, AE 14:115.

incompetence in one's calling. If a man's vocation is that of a biology professor, for example, he had better know a thing or two about DNA, cell division, and the means by which to effectively teach such things to eighteen-year-olds. This takes learning, and so this is the simplest implication of a Lutheran understanding of vocation. But of course Lutheranism's paradoxical nature cannot allow it to be quite as simple as that. As vocations encompass more than paid employment, and include such callings as citizen, husband, and little-league coach, one never in fact has *a single* vocation, but always multiple—and at times perhaps even conflicting—vocations. Any education informed by the Lutheran view, therefore, cannot merely be "vocational" training in the modern sense of the term. It will not aim merely at the development of technicians proficient in a narrow field, but, to revisit two phrases quoted previously, it will aim to develop young men and women "fit for everything," persons who are not merely clever producers and consumers, but who are "wise, honorable, and cultivated citizens." And the only education sufficient to that task is the liberal education. Thus, it has been rightly said that "Lutheran liberal arts is not an oxymoron, but rather an essential statement of the arena in which the character of Lutheran identity is formulated and sustained."[53]

And yet this may not be quite the conception of liberal education about which it is possible to speak in other traditions, as has perhaps become evident. It is true that the reformers could speak, as is often done with reference to liberal education, of learning "for its own sake." Melanchthon, for example, in praising the study of natural philosophy, could write that God "placed in the minds of men the desire of considering things, and the pleasure which accompanies this knowledge. These reasons invite healthy minds to the consideration of nature, *even if no use followed*."[54] Luther similarly speaks of the study of languages; even "if there were no other benefit, . . . this should be enough to delight and inspire us, namely, that they are so fine and noble gifts of God."[55] And yet this notion of learning as its own end, while certainly praised, is never allowed to become the predominate theme in light of the Lutheran emphasis on vocation. Thus is introduced a certain tension in Lutheran speaking about the liberal arts. Indeed, when Luther

53. Simmons, *Lutheran Higher Education: An Introduction*, 22.

54. Quoted in Kusukawa, *The Transformation of Natural Philosophy*, 149–50 (emphasis added).

55. Luther, *To the Councilmen*, AE 45:358. Cf. similarly Luther's *Sermon on Keeping Children in School*, AE 46:243, where he comments on "the pure pleasure a man gets from having studied, even though he never holds an office of any kind."

writes that, "the fine liberal arts, invented and brought to light by learned and outstanding people—even though these people were heathens—are serviceable and useful,"[56] he seems almost blissfully unaware that the most influential of these learned and outstanding heathens would have found oxymoronic his praise of the liberal arts for being useful. Famously discussing the distinction between liberal and servile education, Aristotle had argued that if one "learns anything for his own sake . . . the action will not appear illiberal; but if done for the sake of others, the very same action will be thought menial and servile."[57]

The pursuit of any temporal good for one's own sake, though, sits uncomfortably with a Lutheran view of life. It is, in fact, rather forcefully rejected, as when Luther himself proclaims, "If you find yourself in a work by which you accomplish something good for God . . . or yourself, but not for your neighbor alone, then you should know that the work is *not* a good work."[58] No, he says, the "truly Christian life" is that which "finds expression in works of the freest servitude, cheerfully and lovingly done, with which a man willingly serves another without hope of reward; and for himself he is satisfied with the fullness and wealth of his faith."[59] It is this paradoxical understanding of the Christian's "freest servitude" that stands at the heart of a Lutheran view of life, and so too of learning. And it is this notion which might assuage the sort of fears expressed, for example, by Darryl Hart, when he writes:

> I am haunted by the potential narrowness of a liberal education, since it tempts us to look at students and ourselves merely as minds without bodies, that is, without reference to the families and communities in which we learned to talk, treat others politely, endure eccentric neighbors, root for football teams, and fall in love.[60]

A Lutheran view of life revels like no other in the Christian's liberty, but at the same time emphasizes that this liberty consists in being freed from our sin and our own need of atoning for it—not from our human nature. And by our nature we are placed in societies, cities, and communities amidst neighbors. We are, in the fullest sense, and as that "learned and

56. Plass, *What Luther Says*, no. 1330.

57. Aristotle, *Politics*, 8.2, trans. Benjamin Jowett, 301–2.

58. Quoted in Wingren, *Luther on Vocation*, 120 (emphasis added).

59. Luther, *The Freedom of a Christian*, AE 31:365 (emphasis added, and translation slightly revised).

60. Hart, "Education and Alienation," *Touchstone* 18/8, 35.

outstanding heathen" Aristotle rightly understood, social beings by nature. Being "bound" to our neighbors, then, is in fact being freed to be human precisely as our Lord created us to be.[61] A Lutheran view of learning, therefore, is a view toward being and becoming human, toward cultivating this "freest servitude" and the faith, reason, and virtue robust enough to facilitate faithfully living with its inherently paradoxical tensions.

## Bibliography

Aristotle. *Politics*. Translated by Benjamin Jowett. Mineola: Dover, 2000.

Benne, Robert. "Lutheran View of Christian Humanism." In *Christ and Culture in Dialogue*, edited by Angus J. L. Menuge, 314–22. St. Louis: Concordia Academic, 1999.

Braaten, Carl E. "Foreword." In *Christ and Culture in Dialogue*, edited by Angus J. L. Menuge, 7–13. St. Louis: Concordia Academic, 1999.

Burtchaell, James Tunstead . *The Dying of the Light: The Disengagement of Colleges and Universities from Their Christian Churches*. Grand Rapids: Eerdmans, 1998.

Gengenbach, Constance. "The Secularization of Vocation and the Worship of Work." *The Cresset* 51:2 (December 1987) 5–13.

Gerrish, Brian. *Grace and Reason: A Study in the Theology of Luther*. Oxford: Clarendon, 1962.

Hart, Darryl. "Education and Alienation: What John Henry Newman Could Have Learned from Wendell Berry." *Touchstone* 18:8 (2005) 31–35.

Hughes, Richard Thomas. *The Vocation of the Christian Scholar: How Christian Faith Can Sustain the Life of the Mind*. Grand Rapids: Eerdmans, 2005.

Keen, Ralph. "Introduction." In *A Melanchthon Reader*, edited by Ralph Keen, 1–41. New York: Peter Lang, 1988.

Kittleson, James M. "Luther the Educational Reformer." In *Luther and Learning*, edited by Marilyn J. Harran, 95–114. Selinsgrove, PA: Susquehanna University Press, 1985.

Kusukawa, Sachiko. *The Transformation of Natural Philosophy: The Case of Philip Melanchthon*. Cambridge: Cambridge University Press, 1995.

Luther, Martin. *Luther's Works: American Edition* [hereinafter AE]. 56 vols. Edited by J. Pelikan and H. Lehmann. Philadelphia: Fortress and St. Louis: Concordia, 1955-86.

———. *Commentary on Psalm 101* (1534). AE 13:143–224.

———. *Disputation Against Scholastic Theology* (1517). AE 31:3–16.

———. *Lectures on Genesis* (1535–36). AE 1.

———. "Letter to Eobanus Hessus" (29 March 1523). AE 49:32–35.

———. *An Open Letter to Pope Leo X* (6 September 1520). Prefaced to *The Freedom of a Christian* (1520). AE 31:334–43.

———. "Sermon for the Second Sunday after Epiphany"(17 January 1546). In *D. Martin Luthers Werke: Kritische Gesamtausgabe*, 61 vols., 51:123–34. Weimar: Hermann Bölaus, 1883–1983.

———. *A Sermon on Keeping Children in School* (1530). AE 46:207–58.

61. See Kolb, "Niebuhr's 'Christ and Culture in Paradox' Revisited," 111.

———. *The Small Catechism* (1529). In *The Book of Concord*, edited by Robert Kolb and Timothy J. Wengert, 345–75. Minneapolis: Fortress, 2000.

———. *Table Talk* (Winter, 1542–43). AE 54:452.

———. *To the Christian Nobility of the German Nation Concerning the Reform of the Christian Estate* (1520) AE 44:115–217.

———. *To the Councilmen of All Cities in Germany That They Establish and Maintain Christian Schools* (1524). In AE 45:339–78.

Meilaender, Gilbert. "The Catholic I Am." *First Things* 210 (February 2011) 27–30.

Melanchthon, Philip. *Instructions for the Visitors of Parish Pastors in Electoral Saxony* (1528). AE 40:263–320.

———. "On Correcting the Studies of Youth" (1518). In *A Melanchthon Reader*, edited by Ralph Keen, 47–57. New York: Peter Lang, 1988.

Naugle David K. *Worldview: The History of a Concept*. Grand Rapids: Eerdmans, 2002.

Newman, John Henry, Cardinal. *The Idea of a University*. New York: Image, 1959.

Niebuhr, Richard. *Christ and Culture*. New York: Harper & Brothers, 1951.

Noland, Martin R. "The Lutheran Mind and Its University," *Logia* 17:4 (Reformation 2008) 45–52.

Noll, Mark. "The Lutheran Difference." *First Things* 20 (February 1992) 31–40.

Painter, F. V. N. *Luther on Education*. St. Louis: Concordia, 1928.

Pascal, Blaise. *Pensées*. Translated by A. J. Krailsheimer. New York: Penguin, 1995.

Plass, Ewald, ed. *What Luther Says*. St. Louis: Concordia, 1959.

Simmons, Ernest L. *Lutheran Higher Education: An Introduction*. Minneapolis: Augsburg Fortress, 1998.

Solberg, Richard W. *Lutheran Higher Education in North America*. Minneapolis: Augsburg, 1985.

———. "What Can the Lutheran Tradition Contribute to Christian Higher Education?" In *Models for Christian Higher Education: Strategies for Survival and Success in the Twenty-First Century*, edited by Richard T. Hughes and William B. Adrian, 71–81. Grand Rapids: Eerdmans, 1997.

Spitz, Lewis. "Luther and Humanism." In *Luther and Learning*, edited by Marilyn J. Harran, 69–94. Selinsgrove, PA: Susquehanna University Press, 1985.

———. *The Renaissance and Reformation Movements*. 2 vols. St. Louis: Concordia, 1987.

Weber, Max. *The Protestant Ethic and the Spirit of Capitalism*. Translated by Talcott Parsons. New York: Charles Scribner's Sons, 1958.

Wingren, Gustav. *Luther on Vocation*. Translated by Carl C. Rasmussen. Evansville, IN: Ballast, 1994.

Wright, William J. *Martin Luther's Understanding of God's Two Kingdoms*. Grand Rapids: Baker, 2010.

# CHAPTER FOUR

# A Reformed View of Life and Learning:
# Covenant Epistemology

*Esther Lightcap Meek*

## Introduction

I WILL BEGIN BY sketching key features of a reformational[1] vision of life, which in turn easily suggest its view of learning. Then I want to bring up a matter that has become problematic in this post-Reformation era, both beyond and within the tradition, and that mitigates its authenticity and effectiveness. It is a matter that bears strategically on how we go about life, learning, cultural engagement, and even our Christian discipleship. That matter is epistemology—philosophy about how we know what we know. A defective epistemology has developed beginning in the seventeenth century which continues to grow, dominate and warp Western culture. The reformational tradition includes the lively cry, *semper reformanda!*—always reforming! And while the tradition in the past took steps to address the situation, I believe that the tradition stands in need of further reform. I want to offer a fresh epistemic proposal, and the ever-reforming epistemological therapy it engenders, something I have called covenant epistemology. I argue that covenant epistemology restores the reformational tradition to its intended

---

1. In using the word, "reformational," perhaps more than "Reformed," I follow the practice of some prominent neo-Calvinists such as Albert Wolters. See his *Creation Regained*, 1–2. While the Reformed tradition has its English and Dutch sides (and others, to be sure), and while the Protestant Reformation yielded other denominations besides Presbyterians, my personal sense is that "reformational" suggests especially the lively Kuyperian, or Dutch neo-Calvinian strand, with its forward-looking orientation to redeeming all of life. This is what I present here.

vision and fruit. In light of it, we can imagine some fresh ways to move forward healthily in life and learning, to the end of blessing the nations.

## My entrée into a reformational understanding of life

I became a Calvinist while changing the diapers of my three children. I had grown up a dispensationalist Baptist—one with philosophical questions which, at the time, I felt must be sin. Early exposure to Francis Schaeffer's work showed me that my questions were philosophical.[2] Pursuit of that led me to study with a philosopher who was a student of reformed scholars John Murray and Cornelius Van Til.[3] I married a Presbyterian, and when the children came along I was ever so glad of God's promises to them and us in their baptism.

I have never been much of a lover of small children, but rather a lover of creative thought. Of course they bound my mother's heart irrevocably to each of them, and I believe I was a good mother. I liked them more and more as they got older. But those diaper-changing years grated harshly on my natural inclinations. I continually fought a sense of insignificance. So coming to grasp that my daily work was intrinsically significant proved a critical saving of my morale. I eventually grew to be dying of over-significance.[4]

I was settling in to a reformational vision of life and finding that it changed everything and made it all valuable. Let me list its tell-tale features. First is what I heard called, a strong doctrine of creation. All that God made he made good. He made humans to be his created guests-*cum*-friends, His image bearers, stewards of his world, to make culture, to represent Him to it and it to Him (Genesis 1 and 2). Culture and culture making are good. The formula for work, to express it with a tip of the hat to the one you might remember from high school physics, is as follows: Work is the human energy invested in creation that yields culture. So work is what humans are made to do, and it is good. All work is significant. And I was spared death by over-significance; I decided that that is where calling comes in.

---

2. Schaeffer, *The God Who is There*.

3. That philosopher and theologian, James M. Grier, was the mentor who reshaped the course of my life profoundly. After a massively influential career in teaching and preaching, he recently received promotion to glory.

4. Additionally, I have inhabited denominations which promote exclusively male leadership. In wrestling through the matter of my significance as a female, this Calvinist outlook offered some compensation, so to speak: all of life is religious, all work matters to God.

Discerning calling is domain selection—since we are called to exercise dominion. Humans care for the world together, exercising our diverse array of complementary passions and gifts. God calls me to exercise dominion for a particular domain, together with that diverse community. Not everything is equally significant for me.

Now, Adam's sin led to creation's and culture's bentness; all of it has been bent and ravaged by sin. Humans are culpable; creation is just broken. All of it "needs fixed," as we say in Pittsburgh. Jesus' redemption is for all of life, to redeem all of life.[5] The eschaton, according to Jesus, is the renewal of all things (Matthew 19:28). That is renewal, not replacement. And do not miss the word, all—throughout.

Creation-fall-redemption-restoration (or consummation) is the grand biblical drama or story of redemption. The story does not begin with justification. Redemption means purchasing back what was good and God's to begin with. God does not make any junk, pronounces Albert Wolters, and he does not junk what he makes.[6] That should be our approach, too.

As I went on to argue in a few seminars, God's job description is creating, combating evil, redeeming and restoring; your job description, and mine, images His. You can add preserving and developing (Genesis 2) to the list. Our job description is to do these six things. And, amazingly, God takes our work as his own, signing his name under it the way a master researcher might the work of her or his assistants (Psalm 104). It is as religious to clean my toilet as it is to clean the toilets in the church building. We may indeed whistle while we work.[7]

Such a view directly challenges any divorce between sacred and secular—as per the toilets. All of life is religious. And even if the end time is not exactly what I see now (1 Corinthians 2:9), I can be confident that God loves me to combat evil and redeem and restore my toilet, just because he loves toilets. God cares for the world and culture. Education is our preparation for caring, too.

Through the years, I have been blessed to be alongside a few people in the tradition who have conveyed to me a felt sense of the reformational vision, one that I think is gold. Mostly Dutchmen, they have exuded what I might call, love of dirt. These are all thinkers and philosophers, mind you!

---

5. Frey, et al., *All of Life Redeemed.*

6. Wolters, *Creation Regained.*

7. Meek, "Whistle While You Work"; "Learning to See"; Meek and Williams, *Culture, Work and Calling.*

I have heard aesthetics philosopher Calvin Seerveld tell of his father loving fish and his fish market. Indeed, Seerveld's own writing is earthily, palpably playful, like no one else's.[8] I lived in the Kentucky home of my professor, philosopher Arvin Vos, for some months; he reveled in gardening and building, home care and playing. Bob Heerdt, a financial wizard, a spiritual father of mine in Philadelphia, loves wine making, boat building, tennis and scads of grandchildren, and people like me around the dinner table on Sunday. With Mike Williams, my former theology colleague with whom I taught and wrote, I shared many conversations about theology, philosophy, gardening and house projects. I have seen Dr. Williams, literally, hug a door he made. And he loves fast cars and motorcycles. Philosopher Nicholas Wolterstorff designed and built his own home and majestic shade garden from scratch. I remember a story he told of his uncle, I believe, a cabinet maker, who, when asked to rough up a shack at a farm, could not help but craft exquisitely aligned cabinets. I learned at some point that the great Abraham Kuyper learned his Calvinism from the farmers. These experiences conveyed to me a felt body sense of the reformational vision of life.

This glorious reformational vision thus accords weightiness to creation and culture, to all callings, to stewardly care of the world to the end of the renewal of all things. It therefore values education as preparation for the very thing God has called humans to do in this world, both as humans and as uniquely called individuals. There is no corner of the world and of culture for which education need not prepare us. We cite the injunctions and example of John Calvin and St. Augustine that the stretches of scholarship of even the pagans are good and proper areas which may bless us and in which we are to excel.

However, on this common reformational approach to learning and culture, there are some critical doctrines of Scripture which seem not to get much play. One is, actually, the centrality of Christ's redemption and the redemptive encounter. It is not that redemption is not affirmed. It is more that it does not flavor the vision and its epistemological and academic expression. Redeeming all of life can seem more like a matter of energetic repair.

There is another thing that seems lacking: a kind of intimacy in knowing, a knowing that is communion, and consonant with both wonder and wisdom. Intimacy in knowing certainly accords with Calvin, justly famous as he is for rendering knowing God and knowing self as inextricably intertwined, and speaking as he does of the real, spiritual presence of the Lord

8. Seerveld, *On Being Human.*

in the Sacrament.[9] I intend that my proposals in this talk will address these matters. I intend a reforming of a reformational view of life and learning.

## The matter of antithesis and common grace

People in the reformational tradition share these commitments. But they exhibit a range of responses when it comes to working out what this looks like for Christians with respect to unbelieving culture and unbelieving people. Abraham Kuyper and others spoke of antithesis and common grace.[10] What defines a person fundamentally is her or his heart orientation with respect to God. That orientation is either submission or rebellion. And that heart orientation will shape that person's culture-making. We should expect that the cultural products of unbelievers—in particular, what they take to be true and good—will conflict with those of believers. That is antithesis. On the other hand, we confess that all of life is religious. There is not a square inch of it about which God has not uttered, "Mine!"—Kuyper famously said. The scope of God's lordship and his redemption is worldwide. Plus, God sends the rain on the just and the unjust—he lavishes blessing on all commonly. That blessing includes truth. It also includes the capacity for covenantal commitment in institutions like marriage and government. This has to do with common grace.

Believers have to figure what this means for how they relate to unbelievers and nontheistic cultural institutions. The duality of antithesis and common grace calls forth a spectrum of responses and a continual conversation. Currently in reformed education, antithesis inclines us to emphasize that there is to be a distinctly Christian perspective in all vocations. We have been enjoined to "take every thought captive" to the lordship of Christ (2 Corinthians 10:5). We are to practice scholarship in a Christian perspective, as Wolterstorff expresses it.[11] That means embracing our fundamental commitments with intentionality, and designing research programs growing out of them.

And the emphasis on antithesis has produced the preoccupation with worldviews. A worldview is a framework or lens of our fundamental belief commitments, through which we view everything.[12] Reformed

---

9. Calvin, *Institutes*, 2 vols.

10. Kuyper, *Lectures on Calvinism*.

11. Wolterstorff, "The Mission of the Christian College," 30.

12. Olthuis, "On Worldviews," in *Stained Glass*, 26.

thinkers have associated the nineteenth-century idea of worldview with the commitments and the heart-orientation which the tradition espouses. Creation-fall-redemption-consummation is the Christian worldview.

Apparently because I cut my reformational teeth in a Van Tillian tradition, I have presumed from the beginning that worldview is effectively philosophy, epistemology in particular.[13] Fundamental belief commitments are philosophical, responses to the fundamental philosophical questions: what is real, how do I know, what is right and good, and what does it mean to be human? Thus, philosophical study and awareness is requisite to worldview formation. However, I have come to realize, on a recent re-reading, that Wolters avers that worldview is not philosophy. Worldview, he stipulates, is pretheoretical and is common to all people. But the disciplines of philosophy and theology are specific professional disciplines which are not for everybody. He suggests that worldview is connected with wisdom and with Jesus' concerns. He tacitly implies that philosophy and theology are not.[14] In a way I cannot comprehend or countenance, the reformational tradition can reject the centrality of theology and philosophy to the proper formation and preparation of all stewards.

To presume that the pretheoretical realm of worldview is, by virtue of being pretheoretical, not the proper object of philosophical or theological exploration, is problematic. First, the claim is itself both theological and philosophical. Thus, the position is therefore self-referentially inconsistent, and a sleight of hand, a covert philosophical claim that marginalizes philosophy. The result is damaging and untrue to the reformational "all of life redeemed." The pretheoretical, on this view, does not require the redemptive ministrations of philosophy and theology, and these disciplines do not need to be engaged by all stewards. Third, it allows a philosophically naïve, defective, pretheoretical stance to persist unexamined and adversely to affect all else. It denies to us stewards some important and delightful philosophical resources for reshaping our orientation. And positively, as

13. Cornelius Van Til was the then-new Westminster Theological Seminary's professor of apologetics from its inception in the first part of the twentieth century. He developed a distinctive approach that balanced the antithesis of the Kuyperian tradition with the common grace of the Princetonian tradition. His starting point always merged Christian theology, philosophy and apologetics; to do one was to do the others. There have been a wide spectrum of Van Tillian developments, and they have not always been irenic. Van Til's work has not always been seen as I have seen it, as honoring common grace as thoroughly as it honors antithesis. Van Til's vision continues to salt one side of the reformational tradition.

14. Wolters, *Creation Regained*, 7–10.

will be seen later in this essay, the pretheoretical is just the place for some intriguing and helpful philosophizing.

But even where worldview is properly acknowledged to be philosophical and in need of philosophical ministrations, the emphasis on worldview, in my experience, overdoes antithesis and leaves us unattuned to common grace, or to such a thing as the common good. It can place a too-heavy accent on critique that is unhelpful for youthful college students. It can yield an arrogant suspicion or dismissiveness of neighbors, a restless readiness to criticize, that prevents listening deeply, and loving dirt—as per my Calvinian models. Sadly, we are not so good at a simple delight in the ever-unfolding creation of God and of his intimate presence and self-revelation in it.

Sadly, we are also not so good at realizing that, despite our redemption in Christ, we ourselves, in the already-not yet, remain misoriented to an extent that rivals unbelievers. Also, we may fall short of acknowledging that the cultural products of people in rebellion against the Lord God are only ever partially successful at rebellion; they often voice his praise better than we do. Yet these affirmations follow directly from our reformational commitments. If God is magnetic north, and we are all arrows on the compass, every human is a bent arrow: part of us cannot help but point toward God; part of us resists and bends away. The high ground we are graced through knowing Christ to occupy does not guarantee superior success in our cultural ventures. It does not entitle us to anything but humility and faithfulness as stewards, continually pondering what his ways look like in creation and culture care in this time and place.

I personally take a stance closer to the common grace end of the spectrum. But I propose that we supersede the debate and get on with stewarding by speaking simply of "blessing the nations." When Yahweh set Abraham apart to father his chosen people, part of that blessing and injunction was that in Abraham all nations would be blessed (Gen. 12:1–3). Of course, this promises Christ. It also promises the extension of the Gospel to the Gentiles. But I think it appropriate to take this as a signature of the ways of God that he means us to imitate and to further.

Key to a common grace stance that honors antithesis is a more sophisticated epistemology such as I hope to present here. A revised view of knowing, and also of being, intrinsically enables us to bless the nations.

So while the reformational tradition has offered me a glorious home for all my adult life, and while it calls forth stellar contributions in learning, culture-making and societal care, a few aspects of the way it plays out concern me. To be faithful to the tradition, I believe that we must reform it. And the reform needed is epistemic.

## Epistemic problems the Reformers never knew of

Those adolescent, supposedly sinful, questions of mine included, how do I know there is a material world outside my mind? How do I know that God exists? These are epistemological questions. And they were imbued with the urgency of modernity. I was a Cartesian baby, committed Christian upbringing notwithstanding. It is in the water in the modern Western tradition.

All of us in the West are shaped by the Western tradition of ideas, beginning from Plato (and even earlier) in ancient Greece. St. Augustine and others melded the Greek and the Christian traditions in the centuries after Christ. All of this shapes us just as it did the Reformers.

But beginning with Descartes in the seventeenth century, something new developed which of course they would not have known. That development was modernity, fostered, at its root, by a Cartesian epistemic vision. Descartes' *Cogito, ergo sum*—I think, therefore, I am—birthed the modern self: a pinpoint, disembodied, dislocated, thinking subject, screened off by his own mental activity from the external world, thereby capable of absolute certainty. Besides such "cogitos" existed only a barren external world whose single interesting feature, for Descartes, was its mechanistic measurability.

What Descartes intended as a math-like thought experiment yielded a totalizing vision which proved to shape modernity. It can be connected with the rise of science, the ascendancy of reason known as the Enlightenment, the industrial revolution, modern economics, individualism and mass society—yes, they go together. It can be connected with optimism regarding progress and the future. But while modernist epistemology has engendered immense good, it has simultaneously proved culturally disastrous. In the memorable words of philosopher Marjorie Grene, Descartes stood "on the knife-edge of modernity—on the knife-edge of disaster."[15] What is more, the Cartesian epistemic vision has this way of eliminating all challengers, and also of expanding interminably. "Imperialist" is a great word for it. But by now we have lost much of our optimism regarding the future.

Significant philosophical and cultural challenges have been thrown at this hydra from very soon after its birth. Despite such efforts, however,

15. Grene, *The Knower and the Known*, ch. 3.

modernism survives and grows, fueled by a moral passion for philosophical naturalism, physicalism, or materialism. Ever expanding technology appears to fuel it as well.

How does all this turn up in the water, for all of us? We can glimpse it if we stop to think about how ordinary people generally conceive of what knowledge is. Without any consideration, people generally think that knowledge is facts, data, information, statements and proofs. Acquiring knowledge involves only a linear, passive, transfer of information. We presume that facts and data are accessed through analysis, through a kind of dismembering to get down to individual bits.

Further, we are epistemological dualists. We align knowledge with science, with reason, with the mind, with theory, with objectivity, with abstract concepts, with the public square. We distinguish this privileged cluster from belief, faith, values, emotion, art, embodiment and particularity, from which we strive to purge the privileged member of each binary. I call this our defective epistemic default. It is modernist epistemology.

What makes modernist epistemology destructive, and actually self-destructive, is that this vision also marginalizes essential dimensions of knowing, of being, and of humanness. It sidelines the very covenantal responsibility requisite for good knowing. It occludes knowing's central, transformative dynamic. It depersonalizes knower and known by truncating both severely. It foments disengagement, irresponsibility, indifference, boredom, cluelessness, hopelessness, skepticism, cynicism, atheism, secularism, societal and environmental damage of all sorts. It excludes adventure, confidence, risk, wonder and wisdom.

In his little critique of E.O. Wilson's *Consilience*, called *Life Is a Miracle: An Essay Against Modern Superstition*, renowned writer Wendell Berry refers to this default epistemic presumption as "reductivist epistemology." He fights it tooth and nail, in the name of the lively particularity of covenantal communal membership, cross-disciplinary conviviality in scholarship, and reverent care of the miracle of life. Berry argues that the primary reductionism is to say that knowledge, meaning and experience can be reduced to language. This, he says flatly, is false.[16] Epistemology must honor the more than explainable; to reduce life to the scope of our explanations is to give up on life.[17]

---

16. Berry, *Life is a Miracle*, 151.
17. Ibid., 3, 6–7.

Modernist epistemology is intrinsically atheistic, removing God and the ever-miraculous newness of his involvement in his world. For all that, it is widely acknowledged that Protestant Christianity climbed into bed with modernist epistemology.[18] The Christian church offers no language for doxology, as Old Testament scholar Walter Brueggemann argues, in our "royal consciousness" of Enlightenment-spawned consumerist satiety, no epistemology that accords with the miracle of the resurrection and the imagination of an alternative vision for which we may hope.[19] Missiologist Lesslie Newbigin has famously argued that the West has no ears even to hear the Gospel, due to its defective epistemology. Positively, he argues that the Gospel can only be itself in a plausibility structure of which it alone is the cornerstone.[20] David Kettle, following in Newbigin's footsteps, argues that knowing God and being known by Him must be the paradigm of human knowing and culture; the extant converse, the theoretical paradigm, is a horrendous logical inversion. It has domesticated the church itself, bringing on the Winter of Western Christianity. Epistemology—specifically, for Kettle as for Newbigin, Polanyian epistemology, with which I will acquaint you presently—is key to unleashing the Gospel.[21]

Modernist epistemology has similarly infected the reformational tradition in ways alien to the Reformers' perception. Scholars in the reformational tradition, true to *semper reformanda,* however, did respond epistemologically to the nineteenth-century challenges of higher criticism of Scripture, and of Darwinian evolution, by tapping the then-new idea of worldview, and of presuppositions. It is right to see that this response itself counts as a philosophical challenge to modernist epistemology.[22] It is right to see it as itself a practicing of scholarship in a Christian perspective.

But I believe that, apart from a further epistemological *semper reformanda,* worldview itself succumbs to the defective epistemic default. I

18. Recently it has occurred to me (as a result of reading Fergus Kerr's *Theology after Wittgenstein*) that the Protestant Reformation itself may have been what spawned the modernist worldview. Thus the generally attested belief that conservative Protestantism has imbibed the Cartesian imagination may be to mistake the cause for the effect.

19. Brueggemann, *The Prophetic Imagination,* 50–51.

20. Newbigin, *Proper Confidence.*

21. Kettle, *Western Culture in Gospel Context.* Kettle's book, along with covenant epistemology, as will be seen in this essay, argues the converse as well: that the Gospel is key to unleashing epistemology.

22. This lends further support to my critique of Wolters' understanding of worldview as pretheoretical and thus not philosophical.

find that, under the influence of the still-dominant default of knowledge as information, students cast worldview-formation as an arbitrary, individual choosing of the information you start with. Or they cast worldview as a non-cognitive bias to be minimized as part of objectivity. When worldview and modernist epistemology arm-wrestle, modernist epistemology always wins, and nobody is around to coach the worldview.[23] The unfortunate neo-Calvinian view that worldview is not philosophy, nor the proper subject of its ministrations, insulates worldview, along with the defective default, from reform. It effectively perpetuates the Cartesian vision. It halts epistemic *semper reformanda*. For few recognize, in their concern to challenge dualism, the epistemological dualism that continues to fester deep beneath the surface of our knowing.

Thus, in the reformational tradition, we cannot helpfully talk of learning, let alone Christian discipleship, church and world care, before we address this. The only way to fix the defective epistemic default is first to reveal our desperate, blinding, need of the fix, and then to administer epistemological therapy. Only epistemology of a certain sort does this. But in the process of attending to this matter, we garner a fresh understanding of life and learning, of educating and blessing the nations.

## Covenant epistemology

When I first entered philosophy and the reformational tradition—for me, the one was the other—the fundamental role of presuppositions and worldview seems indisputably obvious to me. It was essential, and central, to do philosophy as the other side of theology. I was learning from Van Tillian theologian John Frame what I felt was a responsible account of biblical parameters of human knowing.[24] But I lacked any purchase on how presuppositions work. Apart from this, they appeared arbitrary. Do I just choose these commitments? And if so, why these and not others? During my PhD studies, I studied plenty of epistemology that seemed dry as dust and unhelpful, but on the side I encountered the work of a twentieth-century Hungarian scientist-turned-philosopher named Michael Polanyi.[25] Polanyi,

---

23. And even among the Reformed philosophers, it seems that the pretheoretical is still cast as non-cognitive, as affective. See, for example, Smith, *Desiring the Kingdom*.

24. Frame, *The Doctrine of the Knowledge of God*.

25. Polanyi, *Personal Knowledge*; *The Tacit Dimension*; *Knowing and Being*.

I came to feel, showed how presuppositions work epistemologically. I have built his core insights into my own covenant epistemology.

According to Polanyi, all knowing, whatever the field, works the same way: we subsidiarily rely on clues integratively to achieve and focus on a coherent pattern. So, for example, when you are reading, you rely subsidiarily on the marks on the page, not focally. You integrate from them to their meaning. When you bike, your felt body sense of balancing is subsidiary. Your focus is (had better be) on getting where you are going. All knowing involves focal awareness responsibly achieved through integration from clues of which we are subsidiarily aware.[26] This means that all knowing is skilled knowing. My Framean gloss on the Polanyian account is to say that those indwelt subsidiary clues consist of three intertwined sectors: the existential (my lived, felt, body sense); the situational (the world, the place of my puzzlement); the normative (any and all authoritative guides and directions, formative traditions, and all theoretical frameworks, including presuppositions). Together they all serve to extend my body into the world, the way any tool does. This very accessible triad of subsidiary clues incorporates into all epistemic acts everything from the Word of God, our fundamental belief commitments or worldview, our language, tradition and community, to our felt body sense and our particular situatedness in place and history. And knowing, engaging the world, is hermeneutical: to be human, and to understand, is to interpret normatively in order to invite the real.

The subsidiary is pretheoretical, inarticulate knowledge (as per Wolters' understanding of worldvew), and so much more: the artful, bodied, situated epistemic "foundation" for all knowing, to be philosophically and in all ways attended to and cultivated. We are not meant to or capable of reducing the subsidiary explicit information. We are, rather, bodily to indwell it with virtuosity—to live it and live from it toward the world. Polanyian subsidiary knowledge makes profound, helpful, sense of worldview, and shows easily how worldview is philosophical, how it is knowing, how it is cross-disciplinarily rich, and how it may be reformed and trained to be skillful. Unlike the currently reformational understanding of worldview, Polanyian subsidiary focal integration is an epistemology which directly challenges the epistemological dualism of modernity, and accomplishes that feat on the level on which alone the therapy must be forwarded: the

---

26. Meek, *Loving to Know*, ch. 4. See also Meek, *Longing to Know*, ch. 6.

level of the pretheoretical, recognized now to be subsidiary.[27] This account makes better sense of wisdom, along with all human knowing, from ordinary to expert.

Subsidiary-focal integration is also heuristic. In a trajectory of coming to know, or discovery (also learning), we scrabble and struggle anticipatively to indwell the clues in such a way that it evokes a coherent, transformative pattern. Successful integration to a coherent pattern unlocks reality's possibilities. My favorite pronouncement of Polanyi's became the focus of my dissertation: "We know we have made contact with reality because we experience a sense of the possibility of unspecifiable future manifestations."[28] This is an epistemology that may restore doxology and the prophetic imagination of alternative visions.

Another great dimension of this approach is that it allows us to recognize the epistemic experience of being on the way to knowing—of anticipative knowing.[29] On the way to knowing, you must rely on clues in your effort to make sense of a puzzlement. The clues include our in articulable sense of a deeper rationality. You only half-understand the significance of clues. You find yourself ever drawn on by unnamable but tantalizing future possibilities. This means that we may be said to know and not know what it is we know—yet. But this feature makes very helpful sense of antithesis and common grace in tandem. For we may cast knowing as a pilgrimage, an unfolding journey in search of insight—one in which even the profoundest epiphany is confirmed by our sense of yet further possibilities. And to cast knowing as pilgrimage is to enable humble common cause of believers and unbelievers, wheat and tares, together. This allows us to bless the nations, as well as being blessed by them.

We also may expect that our insight changes us. Knower and all clues are transformed as reality graciously self-discloses and breaks in. Knowing changes the knower. Every "Aha! moment" grows us in personhood and in epistemic maturity. That actual "aha!" epiphany is encounter. The act of coming to know, of insight or discovery, is a lively, personally engaged,

---

27. The defective epistemic default we have all inherited has been subsidiarily operative. One thing I have always appreciated about the Polanyian account is that subsidiaries are not thereby correct or immune from revision. It is just that revising them, since they are subsidiary, involves a complexity that myopically proposition-based epistemologies fail to account for.

28. For example, Polanyi, *Personal Knowledge*, vii–viii. Meek, *Contact With Reality*.

29. Meek, *Loving to Know*, ch. 6, and txt. 4.

dance of mutuality unfolding relationally between knower and yet-to-be-known.[30] This is an epistemology of transformation.

This epistemology radically reshapes how we see reality. Reality itself no longer is re-visioned into two-dimensional ones and zeros, nor we into automatons. It is no longer suspected, and it is no longer passive. Our loving to know confers dignity and freedom that invites reality itself, including God, ever to come surprisingly and transformatively in newness. Reality is gift, as theologian Philip Rolnick and others aver.[31] Reality comes in newness, akin to the descent of God. Reverend John Ames, in Marilynne Robinson's *Gilead*, writes, "Wherever you turn your eyes the world can shine like transfiguration. You do not have to bring a thing to it except a little willingness to see."[32] As Colin Gunton argues, Polanyian epistemology restores the healing relationality with nonhuman creation which our society and culture so desperately needs.[33] Knowing is itself an orientation to being that invites wonder with every wooing of the real. It is an invitation to an unfolding dance of relationship in which knower and known bring mutual blessing and healing. Rather than knowing in order to love, we love in order to know.

In these features of knowing cast on Polanyian lines, I have come to discern "hints of interpersonal reciprocity." Thus I have developed covenant epistemology.[34] Covenant epistemology contends that the paradigm of knowing is, most fundamentally, not impersonal theory, but interpersonal, covenantally constituted, relationship between knower and yet-to-be-known, to the end of, not comprehensive, static, absolute information, but rather, more dynamically objective and ongoing communion.

To cast knowing as a transformative event which occurs in mutuality, binding knower and known in an unfolding relationship, allows us to begin to tap the Gospel epistemologically. We may take the redemptive encounter, liturgically reenacted in the Eucharist, as the paradigm of knowing. Every "Aha! moment" thus prototypes and signposts the coming of the Lord.[35]

---

30. All these phrases, from thinkers John Macmurray, Martin Buber, James Loder, and Colin Gunton, I explore in *Loving to Know*.

31. Rolnick, *Person, Grace, and God*; Meek, *Loving to Know*.

32. Robinson, *Gilead*, 245.

33. Gunton, *The One, the Three, and the Many*.

34. *Loving to Know* constitutes my development of and case for covenant epistemology.

35. James Loder argues this in *The Transforming Moment*.

To know him is to be known by him, as Calvin said, to know ourselves and the world, together with others in pilgrimage with whom we are joyously, covenantally, bound. Knowing on this paradigm is fraught with the sweet (and terrifying) intimacy of abiding in Christ.

Covenant epistemology calls us to knowing for shalom. On this account, insight transforms both knower and known. Our knowing should move the world in the direction of shalom. Knowing should be therapeutic. This connects knowing integrally with the cultural mandate. And in our own lives, once we understand that knowing is transformation, not mere information, once we ourselves have been transformed, we become *semper transformanda*, catalysts of ongoing transformation. Epistemological etiquette, as I call it, orients us in blessing toward God and His world. It is the epistemic posture of blessing the nations. The posture itself invites blessing. The Christians' prophetic ministry to this world may, and must, include, epistemic reorientation.

## Inviting the real

Thus, covenant epistemology taps redemption in a far richer, more Calvinian, way than has the recent reformational tradition. As education guru Parker Palmer writes, the shape of our epistemology is the shape of our lives.[36] We need to let the redemptive encounter, and the mutuality of covenantally constituted interpersonal relationship of knower and known in knowing, epistemically shape our lives and learning.

Covenant epistemology implies that we should cast all our efforts to know as efforts to "invite the real." Inviting the real involves a posture that humbly welcomes and embraces the risk of the gracious, lively incursion of the real. It is the posture of the Hebrews, according to Rabbi Abraham Joshua Heschel, to which we should aspire: where the Greeks learn in order to comprehend, the Hebrews learn in order to be apprehended.[37] What we may not wrest indifferently in a robot-like, indifferent, harvesting of "factoids"—in which the known hardly can be said to self-disclose truthfully—we may hope in grace to have revealed to us—truthfully—as we behave properly, personally, hospitably. We must practice epistemological etiquette—good epistemic practice—to invite the real.

---

36. Palmer, *To Know as we are Known*, 21.

37. This is the paraphrase of my colleague, Robert Frazier.

The following are five loci of covenant epistemology's lengthy catalog of epistemic practices.[38]

1. First and foremost is *love.* We do not know in order to love; rather, we love in order to know. We promise to love, honor and obey so as to invite the gracious self-disclosure of the other. We love in hope of understanding. And understanding must be rendered more on the lines of communion rather than exhaustive information. Love is the central, all encompassing, epistemic practice. As author Annie Dillard, Episcopal priest/cook Robert Farrar Capon, and Christian mystic Simone Weil all emphasize, it is the lover who sees.[39]

2. Second, composure. We compose ourselves as knowers. In fact, we grow as knowers as we are known by the real in its gracious inbreaking. Every little "Aha! moment" grows us. Every healthy interpersonal encounter grows us. As we mature in the care and noticing regard of others, we are composed, and we become better at knowing. Robert Pirsig, in his hippie-era classic, *Zen and the Art of Motorcycle Maintenance,* argues that the main ingredient it takes to fix a motorcycle is peace of mind.[40] That is composure!

3. Third, comportment. Comportment involves binding yourself covenantally to live life on the terms of the yet-to-be-known. It involves something like hospitable welcome, a vulnerable openness, a readiness to listen deeply.[41] It involves exercising trust, obedience, humility, and patience toward the not-yet-known. This seems to me to be the opposite of critical analysis, which proves to be dismissive and unhearing. It does presume the worth of the effort, the goodness of reality. Why would reality disclose itself to suspicion?

4. Fourth, strategy—of an intimate, connected, empathetic sort. We must put ourselves in the place where insight is likely to come. This involves the responsible, pledge-like, sacrificial, investment of ourselves in practice or study before we are even in a position to apprehend the real. And we must exercise the kind of noticing regard that confers dignity on the yet-to-be-known. We must delight; delight, says David

38. Meek, *Loving to Know,* ch. 15.

39. Dillard, *Pilgrim at Tinker Creek;* Capon, *The Supper of the Lamb;* Simone Weil, *Waiting for God,* 92.

40. Pirsig, *Zen and the Art of Motorcycle Maintenance,* 294–97; also chs. 6 and 7.

41. Steiner, *Real Presences,* 137–56.

Bentley Hart, is the premise of any sound Christian epistemology.[42] We must listen indwellingly—meaning, trying to get inside the thing we are trying to understand. Nobel Prize-winning geneticist Barbara McClintock has said that her best epistemic practice involved listening to the ear of corn, having a feeling for the organism.[43]

5. Finally, communion. The goal of our knowing is itself a best epistemic practice. Our epistemic goal is friendship with God and his world. Understanding a computer or a dog issues in delightful, ongoing, perichoretic (that means dance-like) knowing and being known.[44] Since communion is both goal and practice, the Eucharist, liturgically reenacting our redemptive encounter with Christ, additionally becomes great schooling for inviting the real. The Gospel breaks open our world by integrating us transformatively into the Lord's.[45] Communion is the seat of ongoing wonder and growing wisdom. [/NL 1-5]

## Implications for learning and higher education

I commend to you that we let covenant epistemology shape our understanding of learning, and of what higher education should seek to cultivate in young lives. Laying it alongside our academic efforts, we can properly accredit best epistemic practices, and start to be more intentional about them.

First, we must offer epistemological therapy. Our deeply entrenched defective epistemic default with its generally undetected epistemological dualism is going to take explicit and continual challenging for us to expect our students, and our academic structures, to overcome. Nothing less than Western culture, the proper grasp of the Gospel, and the shape the church and its mission is at stake.

Second, we must devise some concrete way, as a Christian institution, without inappropriately trying to be a church, to render the redemptive

---

42. Hart, *The Beauty of the Infinite*, 253.

43. Referenced by Palmer in *The Courage to Teach*, 55–56.

44. The Cappadocian Church Fathers (and mothers, according to church historian Les Fairfield) deemed perichoresis the dynamic movement of the Holy Trinity. Meek, *Loving to Know*.

45. David Kettle utilizes Polanyian subsidiary-focal integration to elaborate his account of the Gospel as "the approach of God as our ultimate context." *Western Culture in Gospel Context*. See also Meek, "Review of David J. Kettle, *Western Culture in Gospel Context*," 74–76.

encounter with Christ the central epistemic practice. Of course, covenant epistemology inculcates that vision and forms us in being intentional about it. But I imagine we could intentionally develop creative strategies that underscore and actually embody the orientation. It might involve accredited space for reflection and prayer to invite the real—to invite Him. It might involve voiced gratitude and worship—with these always underscored as being the very trajectory of inviting the real in all knowing. It might involve a liturgical context for class. We must hold the doxological (worship) and the doxastic (belief) together, says my philosophy colleague, Dr. Robert Frazier. Indeed, I believe that you could leave the curriculum unchanged (except for covenant epistemology) and continually invent fresh ways to center class and study around worship. This might prove to be something like a monastery. But monasteries, after all, saved Western culture.

Third, excellence in information is important, but we must teach and model before students that we temporarily focus on it so as to indwell it subsidiarily. We love in order to know. We collect data because we love. We climb into the information subsidiarily in caring pursuit of a vision. The goal of education is not information; the goal is connoisseurship—intimate communion with the real—to the end of shalom. Knowing is transformative insight, the graced inbreaking of reality in response to our patient ministrations. We must educate for insight and thus for shalom.[46]

Fourth, we must design and assess our academic efforts with a view to their effectiveness in forming students as candidates to invite the real. We must teach and cultivate epistemological etiquette—love, composure, comportment, strategy and communion. We may redo the stresses (in the sense of accents) of our curriculum and pedagogy and assessed outcomes to accord with these practices. We must see our efforts as first of all bringing students to the epistemic posture of lovers responsibly inviting the real. We must inspire love of the yet to be known—the kind of love that covenantally embraces risk in the pursuit.

Fifth, we may relativize the significance of the specific curriculum we offer. Covenant epistemology removes from curricular decisions the severe ultimacy which the theoretical paradigm inappropriately lays on it. In the process, this actually both frees and heightens the curriculum's value by rendering it subsidiary.[47] Understanding is not about an exact "content."

46. Wolterstorff's titular phrase, "education for shalom," inspired covenant epistemology's "knowing for shalom."

47. Fixating on the focal issues in behavior and consequences akin to what Scripture

We must study, not the content focally, so much as what it means to indwell the content subsidiarily, in submission to a farther, as yet half-understood focus. Also, it is critical to study and indwell content in areas beyond our field of expertise. To excel in our disciplines, we must study beyond them. Integrative patterns meld a dynamic and unspecifiable array of subsidiaries drawn from a wide array of disciplines. This assigns profound value to a diversity in the core as well as to any kind of intentional creative cross-disciplinary syntheses. Subsidiary-focal integration helps us value apprenticeship in a larger tradition of the liberal arts as a time-honored cultivation of our humanness and culture.

In academic work, sixth, we should cultivate conviviality. Knowing as subsidiary-focal integration, and as inviting the real, enjoins what Michael Polanyi called conviviality—a society of explorers in the covenantally trusting, joyous, fellowship of conversation as the best means to insight. This begins with the ever-critical convivial conversation among colleagues. Then students join in relational apprenticeship with their teachers and other fellow learners, convivially to invite the real. This is the living dynamic which interdisciplinary courses may model and implement.

Seventh, we must be intentional about the pedagogical relationship. If covenant epistemology renders curriculum subsidiary, it foregrounds the pedagogical relationship. For the teacher must teach, not so much the curricular items, as her- or himself. The teacher must teach him- or herself engaging the subject covenantally, hospitably, in love. To teach is to model attending in love, indwelling the clues, to invite the real. The noticing regard, the attentive gaze of the face of the one who loves both the subject and the student, is a powerful catalyst to insight. Teachers, by the way, include the authors of great books to which we apprentice ourselves. We must learn, as Martin Buber writes, how to be addressed by a book.[48]

Eighth, we must underscore wonder and wisdom. Francis Bacon inaugurated modernity by casting knowledge as the elimination of wonder. Wisdom has also found no place in an information-based epistemology. But covenant epistemology accredits, not "unbridled lucidity," as Polanyi panned it, but the mystery that is the deepest understanding of reality and our communion with it. It restores knowing to being intrinsically a

---

describes as idolatry. Rendering knowledge as subsidiary helpfully addresses this and frees us to proper humanness. Of course fixation on the focal characterizes modernist epistemology, giving warrant for concern for modern culture.

48. Buber, *I and Thou*, 38.

trajectory from wonder to wisdom. Wisdom is the maturation of our wonder. On this account, the business of higher education is freer to be about the cultivation of humanness, wonder and wisdom.

On this account, higher education is freer to be about love. We cultivate lovers who know for shalom. Higher education, ninth, is to cultivate lovers, people who love in order to know, who know (in the very act, intrinsically) for shalom. As Robert Farrar Capon argues, we should be amateurs—lovers—loving things as they are, as God does (and "man was not made in God's image for nothing"), and in that loving gaze, look the world back to grace.[49] Inviting the real offers openness to the world and others, it nurtures a reverent, hospitable, shalomish relationship with creation, culture and society. Covenant epistemology is what I call *semper transformanda*—always transforming. It replaces a death-producing epistemic paradigm with a dynamic, lively one that heals knowers and knowing. It renders us able to "know for shalom," to bring healing to the known as well. Higher education is to cultivate our posture and our readiness to invite the real, to know for shalom, to bless the nations.

Part of this blessing, according to David Kettle, must be epistemological therapy. Colleges in the reformational tradition may aspire to blessing the church and blessing the nations through reorienting students epistemologically. Such a reorientation readmits doxology into knowing, and openness to imagine and invite newness and miracle in reality. In this, says my colleague Bob Frazier, colleges exercise rightly their prophetic role—the very prophetic imagination to which Brueggemann summons the people of God. So, tenth, our colleges and students may bless the nations with epistemological reorientation and common grace covenantal collaboration.

Finally, our philosophy of education must honor the classroom as holy. Where this is our agenda in higher education, the classroom community is indeed a burning bush, on whose holy ground we take off our shoes.[50] This is a richer reformational vision of life and learning, one more philosophically attuned, and more deeply consistent with its formative professed commitments.

---

49. Capon, *Supper of the Lamb*, 3–5.

50. Seerveld, *Rainbows*.

## Conclusion

Philosopher James K. A. Smith honored my book, *Loving to Know,* with an endorsement, in which he describes me as putting my own stamp on the reformational tradition. In this essay you can see what he may mean. I have argued that covenant epistemology is that which revitalizes the tradition by being truer to the tradition than other developments may have been. It rescues it from deadness incurred by a hidden, toxic epistemology, and unleashes it to exciting future prospects as we engage and invite the ever-new real, to know for shalom and to bless the nations. This vision reorients us concretely to the dynamic and gracious inbreaking of God. It situates life and learning as the very table of God's presence, to which we and all others may be welcomed.[51]

## Bibliography

Berry, Wendell. *Life is a Miracle: An Essay Against Modern Superstition.* Berkeley: Counterpoint, 2000.

Bradshaw Frey, et al. *All of Life Redeemed: Biblical Insight for Daily Obedience.* Brescia: Paedeia, 1983.

Brueggemann, Walter. *The Prophetic Imagination.* 2nd ed. Minneapolis: Fortress, 2001.

———. *Truthtelling as Subversive Obedience.* Edited by K. C. Hanson. Eugene, OR: Cascade, 2011.

Buber, Martin. *I and Thou.* Translated by Walter Kaufmann. New York: Charles Scribner's Sons, 1970.

Calvin, John. *Institutes of the Christian Religion.* Edited by John T. McNeill. Translated by Ford Lewis Battles. Library of Christian Classics. 2 vols. Philadelphia: Westminster, 1960.

Capon, Robert Farrar. *The Supper of the Lamb: A Culinary Reflection.* New York: Harcourt Brace Jovanovich, 1967.

Dillard, Annie. *Pilgrim at Tinker Creek.* New York: HarperCollins, 1974.

Frame, John. *The Doctrine of the Knowledge of God.* Phillipsburg, NJ: P&R, 1987.

Grene, Marjorie. *The Knower and the Known.* University of California, 1974.

Gunton, Colin. *The One, the Three, and the Many.* Cambridge: Cambridge University Press, 1993.

Hart, David Bentley. *The Beauty of the Infinite.* Grand Rapids: Eerdmans, 2003.

Kerr, Fergus, O.P. *Theology after Wittgenstein,* 2nd ed. London: SPCK, 1997.

Kettle, David J. *Western Culture in Gospel Context: Towards the Conversion of the West; Theological Bearings for Mission and Spirituality.* Eugene, OR: Cascade, 2011.

Kuyper, Abraham. *Lectures on Calvinism.* Grand Rapids: Eerdmans, 1943.

---

51. Thanks to my colleague, Robert Frazier, for insightful comments on a draft of this paper.

Loder, James. *The Transforming Moment*. 2nd ed. Colorado Springs: Helmers and Howard, 1989.

Meek, Esther L. "Contact With Reality: An Examination of Realism in the Thought of Michael Polanyi." PhD diss., Temple University, 1983.

———."Learning to See." Junior High Youth Retreat, Twin Oaks PCA Church (Fall 2001).

———. *Longing to Know: The Philosophy of Knowledge for Ordinary People*. Grand Rapids: Brazos, 2003.

———. *Loving to Know: Introducing Covenant Epistemology*. Eugene, OR: Cascade, 2011.

———. "Review of David J. Kettle, *Western Culture in Gospel Context: Towards the Conversion of the West; Theological Bearings for Mission and Spirituality*." *Tradition and Discovery: The Polanyi Society Journal* (34:1, 2012–13) 74–76.

———. "Whistle While You Work." Evenings at the Institute (Covenant Seminary), Borders Bookstore (October 2000).

———, and Michael D. Williams, *Culture, Work and Calling*. Class for Covenant Theological Seminary, St. Louis, MO, 1998–2002.

Olthuis, James . "On Worldviews." In *Stained Glass: Worldview and Social Science*, edited by Paul A. Marshall et al., 26–40. Lanham MD: University Press of America, 1989.

Newbigin, Lesslie. *Proper Confidence: Faith, Doubt and Certainty in Christian Discipleship*. Grand Rapids: Eerdmans, 1995.

Palmer, Parker. *The Courage to Teach: Exploring the Inner Landscape of a Teacher's Life*. San Francisco: Jossey-Bass, 1998.

———. *To Know as We Are Known: Education as a Spiritual Journey*. San Francisco: Harper, 1966.

Pirsig, Robert M. *Zen and the Art of Motorcycle Maintenance: An Inquiry into Values*. New York: Morrow, 1974.

Polanyi, Michael. *Knowing and Being: Essays by Michael Polanyi*. Edited by Marjorie Grene. Chicago: University of Chicago Press, 1969.

———. *Personal Knowledge: Towards a Post-Critical Philosophy*. Corrected ed. Chicago: University of Chicago Press, 1962.

———. *The Tacit Dimension*. Foreword by Amartya Sen. Chicago: University Press, 2009.

Robinson, Marilynne. *Gilead*. New York: Picador, 2006.

Rolnick, Phillip. *Person, Grace, and God*. Grand Rapids: Eerdmans, 2007.

Schaeffer, Francis A. *The God Who is There*, Evanstown: InterVarsity, 1968.

Seerveld, Calvin. *On Being Human: Imaging God in the Modern World*. Burlington, Ontario: Welch, 1988.

———. *Rainbows for a Fallen World*. Toronto: Tuppence, 1980.

Smith, James K. A. *Desiring the Kingdom: Worship, Worldview, and Cultural Formation*. Grand Rapids, MI: Baker Academic, 2009.

Steiner, George. *Real Presences*. Chicago: University of Chicago Press, 1989.

Weil, Simone. *Waiting for God*. Translated by Emma Craufurd. New York: HarperCollins, 2001.

Wolters, Albert M. *Creation Regained: Biblical Basics for a Reformational Worldview*, 2nd ed. Grand Rapids: Eerdmans, 1985.

Wolterstorff, Nicholas. "The Mission of the Christian College at the End of the Twentieth Century." In *Educating for Shalom: Essays on Christian Higher Education*, edited by Clarence W. Joldersma and Gloria Goris Stronks, 24–35. Grand Rapids, MI: Eerdmans, 2004.

# CHAPTER FIVE

# An Anglican View
# of Life and Learning:
# Grace and Gratitude

*Ashley Null*

ANYONE ATTEMPTING TO DESCRIBE Anglicanism's distinctive view of human life which informs its vision of liberal learning is immediately confronted with three interdependent questions, each decidedly disputed in its own right. Firstly, is there such a thing as Anglicanism? Secondly, whatever Anglicanism is, is there really something distinctive about it? Thirdly, how does this Anglicanism understand the liberal tradition with respect to learning? We will consider each question in turn.

First, consider a paradigmatic scene from July 1539. Recently loosed from papal authority five years before, the newly self-governing Church of England had began the painful process of deciding for itself what it thought was the Gospel truth. After an initial movement in the direction of Lutheranism, though clearly never fully embracing Luther, the Crown in parliament has just charted a decidedly different course. The new Act of Six Articles tacked back to a much more medieval understanding of salvation and the sacraments.

At this moment in Anglican history, Ralph Morice, Archbishop Cranmer's principal private secretary, was caught in a throng of rowboats jammed together between the king's barge and the bear-baiting entertainment on the bank of the Thames. Wedged between royal authority and controlled violence, all seemed normal. But then suddenly, "within one *pater noster*," everything changed. The violence was no longer leashed. The bear broke its chain and sought relief in the water. The dogs followed in pursuit. All the animals then headed towards Morice's boat. There was anger, mayhem and no room to manoeuvre. Morice's companions, yeomen of the guard, abandoned ship. Some leapt onto neighbouring barges. A couple missed their target, landing directly in the water. Like his master after the passage of the Act of Six Articles, Morice just stayed put, even as all the commotion flooded the rowboat with water, even as the bear, "seekying as it were, ayde and succour of hym" reared up on its hind legs directly in front of him. As he, still in the boat, twisted himself back out of harm's way, even greater harm came. The fair copy of Cranmer's latest missive for the king, the brief outlining at Henry's request the arguments the archbishop had used to dispute the Six Articles for three days in Parliament, the copy which he had written out for Cranmer and had not dare leave unattended back in his room at Lambeth Palace, the manuscript which he had strapped to his waist for safe-keeping, that strictly confidential memorandum was now flung by all the commotion out upon the waters, streaming out of Morice's reach. He called to Princess Elizabeth's bear keeper to pick it up. A traditionalist, the bearward did so, but then had a conservative priest standing on the bank immediately read it. When he learned from the priest the brief's contents, he refused to give it back to Morice. Rather, the bear keeper intended to give the treatise to Stephen Gardiner or another of Cranmer's theological opponents in order to do maximum damage to the evangelical cause. Terror for one's life instantly metamorphosed into terror for one's life's work, which undoubtedly merely reinforced terror for one's life—such topsy-turvy chance changes in circumstances must have seemed the lot of an English evangelical's life, as long as it lasted, in mid-Tudor times. Eventually, Morice got Thomas Cromwell, Henry's chief counsellor, to pry the brief from the bear keeper's grip before any real damage could be done. The story ends with Cranmer smiling at Morice and telling him that since both the brief and its bearer had been through the wash, he should go back and write a new fair copy.[1]

While quite comical, the vignette also powerfully reveals the issues at the very heart of Anglican identity: competing factional visions for the church's self-understanding with an ultimate reliance on governmental intervention to decide the question. It is a scene that will be played out again and again in Anglican history, for up until the 1950s Anglicanism was a

---

1. Foxe, *Actes and Monuments*, 1355–56.

thoroughly Erastian institution, and this yeast still leavens many of the issues facing its world-wide fellowship today.

Yet we dare not neglect one further significant detail in the story which is usually overlooked in all that splashing about. As a throwaway line summarizing the brief's content, Morice gives us the first explicit reference to that famous triad of Anglican theological authorities:

> The Archbishop collectyng both his arguments, authorities of Scriptures, and Doctors together, caused hys Secretarie to write a fayre booke therof for the king, after this order. First the Scriptures were alledged, then the Doctours, thirdlye folowed the Argumentes deducted from those authorities.[2]

In other words, in the midst of the uncertainties of this time, the theological method on which Cranmer relied to advance the evangelical cause in his day was nothing other than an appeal to Scripture, tradition and reason. Although its use by Richard Hooker at the end of the Sixteenth Century would enshrine the triad as the essence of Anglicanism, Hooker was not the first sixteenth-century English Protestant to do so.[3] Cranmer himself had already established the precedent that Anglican beliefs and practices must be defined and justified by a combination of Scripture, tradition and reason. What will demarcate the fault lines in the future development of the Church of England will be the differing weight the competing factions will attribute to each authority. Let's take at look.

## Part I: The Development of Anglicanisms

### The first phase of Anglicanism: The Sixteenth-Century Reformed Church

With Edward VI's accession in 1547, the Church of England turned decisively Protestant. Thomas Cranmer firmly held to the principle that Scripture had to interpret itself through the Augustinian/Erasmian technique of

2. Ibid., 1355.

3. Note, however, that Hooker's preferred descending order of authority was Scripture, reason and then tradition: "[W]hat scripture doth plainelie deliver, to that first place both of creditt and obedience is due; the next whereunto is whatsoever anie man can necessarelie conclude by force of reason; after these the voice of the Church succeedeth"; *Laws* (V.8.2) in *Folger Edition*, 2.39.8–11.

the collation of passages, i.e., more difficult ones being understood in the light of more clear ones.[4] Yet, he was equally adamant that any resulting authentic exegesis could never be novel in the history of the church. While he did not seek to establish and follow a patristic consensus, he did insist on some prior stream of patristic witness as confirmation that any biblical interpretation had been validly derived from *sola scriptura*.[5] In short, Cranmer saw Scripture as Polaris, that fixed and certain unmovable guide by which Christians should orient their lives. However, tradition and reason remained necessary auxiliary stars, which when lined up would helpfully point to the Bible's own position. Therefore, the Anglican formularies issued under his guidance sought to bring the Church of England gradually, but steadily, into doctrinal conformity with reformed Continental Protestantism.

The *Book of Homilies* (1547) for parish clergy taught *sola scriptura* and justification by faith. The first *Book of Common Prayer* (1549) insisted on English as the language of the liturgy, restored systematic reading of Scripture and removed all references to both personal merit and the mass as a propitiatory sacrifice. The revised, second *Book of Common Prayer* (1552) went even further than the first, making clear that Christ's eucharistic presence was spiritual in nature, a holy communion in the heart of the believer through personal faith. Lastly, the Forty-Two Articles (1553) compiled an authoritative list of the Edwardian church's application of reformed scriptural exegesis to the controversial issues of its day, including predestination.

At the death of Edward 1553 a five-year interlude during the reign of Mary Tudor followed when the Church of England was restored to Roman obedience. However, Elizabeth ascended to the throne in 1558 and turned the clock back to the clearly Protestant ethos of Edward's reign. In 1559 Parliament declared the Queen to be supreme governor and reissued both the 1547 *Book of Homilies* and a slightly amended 1552 *Book of Common Prayer*. In 1563 the bishops also approved a new, second *Book of Homilies* and the revision of the Forty-Two articles into Thirty-Nine. The minor changes between the Edwardian and Elizabethan formularies were towards a more comprehensive Protestantism that would be less offensive to Lutherans. For example, the 1549 words of administration in Holy Communion permitted a real presence understanding of the sacrament. The 1552 words

---

4. Null, "Official Tudor Homilies," 353–57.

5. Null, "Princely Marital Problems and the Reformers' Solutions," 146–49. Cf. Quantin, *The Church of England and Christian Antiquity*, 24–27, 31–34.

clearly emphasized commemoration. Elizabeth's 1559 Prayer Book simply combined them. If you have only a passing familiarity with Anglicanism, you will most likely have been told that the Elizabethan Church represented a comprehensive settlement consciously trying to include as wide a spectrum of theological beliefs as possible. Current scholarship, however, now agrees that the Sixteenth-Century Church of England was committed to a moderate, generous reformed theology, a *via media* not between Rome and Geneva but between Wittenberg and Geneva.[6] Perhaps nothing makes clear the untenable nature of the old canard of Elizabethan comprehensiveness as the constant diatribe against Roman Catholic idolatry in the second *Book of Homilies*. Remember, these sermons were required reading in the vast majority of English parish every Sunday just as much as the prayer book. Perhaps the most gratuitous expression of this official weekly diatribe against medieval practices comes in the homily on keeping the church clean:

> And forasmuch as your churches are scoured and swept from the sinful and superstitious filthiness wherewith they were defiled and disfigured, do ye your parts, good people, to keep your churches comely and clean: suffer them not to be defiled with rain and weather, with dung of doves and owls, stares, and choughs, and other filthiness, as it is foul and lamentable to behold in many places of this country.[7]

In other words, Roman Catholic devotional practices and bat guano are equally filthy in God's eyes.

And what was the source of such idolatrous practices? According to the *Second Book of Homilies*, a medieval failure to get the right relationship between reason and Scripture. The scholastics had erred because "they sought not the will of God but rather the will of reason."[8] Therefore,

> reason must give place to God's Holy Spirit; you must submit your worldly wisdom and judgment unto his divine wisdom and judgment. Consider that the Scripture, in what strange form soever it be pronounced, is the word of the living God.[9]

6. See Wallace, "*Via Media?* A Paradigm Shift," 72, 2–21.

7. Griffiths, *The Two Books of Homilies*, 278.

8. Ibid., 488.

9. Ibid., 377.

Clearly, the Sixteenth-Century Church of England was firmly committed to the supremacy of Scripture for its faith and practice.

### The Second Phase of Anglicanism:
### The Seventeenth-Century Caroline Divines

As exemplified by Lancelot Andrewes, William Laud and Jeremy Taylor, the theologians favoured by King Charles I and King Charles II consciously rejected the reformed ethos of the Elizabethan church. Instead, beginning with their leadership of worship at Westminster Abbey and the cathedrals but gradually spreading throughout the land, the Caroline divines shaped Anglicanism as something free from both Roman and Protestant "innovations." For them, the Church of England's doctrine was expressed, not by the homilies or the articles, but by the prayers and ancient creeds in its liturgy. Seeking to their vision was a church where bishops as well as kings were divinely instituted, where grace flowed primarily through the sacraments, where the liturgy was to be performed with as much heavenly splendour as possible, and human wills strove to co-operate with sacramental grace so as to lead holy lives. Their commitment to the "holiness of beauty" was the genesis of what many later commentators would call "Classical Anglicanism." Committed to repristinating the belief and practices of the undivided church, the Caroline divines insisted that both the interpretation of Scripture and theological reasoning had to been in accordance with the consensus of the Fathers.

With the outbreak of civil war in 1642, both Laud (1645) and Charles I (1649) were executed, episcopacy abolished and prayer book Anglicanism proscribed. When the monarchy was eventually restored in 1660, Charles II (1630–85) also restored the Anglican Church of his father, including a new *Book of Common Prayer* moderately revised along Laudian lines (1662). Consequently, nearly 3000 Puritan clergy left the state system.

### The Third Phase of Anglicanism:
### Latitudinarianism

The Glorious Revolution deposed Charles II's Roman Catholic brother James II after only three years on throne in 1688. Some four hundred Anglican clergy, including the Archbishop of Canterbury, left the church, since their belief in the divine institution of kings and bishops would not allow them to swear an oath to the new sovereigns. Wearied by more than two decades of strife with the Reformed clergy who had left the Church of England upon the return of the prayer book, the new government passed the Act of Toleration (1689) that permitted with certain restrictions Trinitarian Protestants who dissented from the established Anglican parochial system to gather legally their own worshipping communities.

Having already lost those clergy who were most committed to Reformed Protestantism and now the most dedicated to the principles of the undivided church as well, the Whig leadership of the Anglican Church after the Glorious Revolution increasingly found its inspiration in the prevailing intellectual principles of the Enlightenment. As a result, the triumvirate of theological authority was reprioritized by such leading thinkers as Archbishop John Tillotson (1630–94) and John Locke (1632–1704). Now the search for simplicity of doctrine and the necessity of morality was begun through reason, whose conclusions then evaluated Scripture and church tradition. Moreover, reason itself was understood anew, as an autonomous, impartial judge, unlike reason in Cranmer and the Caroline Divines which was to be aided by grace and devotion. Guided by reason's objective power, religion became merely a matter of conduct based on the simple truths of Nature, or in the memorable title of Matthew Tindale's influential book, a *Christianity as old as the Creation.*[10] The end result was a church in the Eighteenth Century whose chief purpose was to inculcate personal morality so as to maintain public order.

## The Fourth Phase of Anglicanism:
## The Three Streams of the Nineteenth-Century Church

During three parties of the Church of England emerged, each applying to the primacy of one of the theological authorities and a previous century as the basis for its claim to be the true Anglican Church.

The *Low Church Evangelicals* preached a return to the Sixteenth-Century reformed formularies with their insistence on the supremacy of Scripture, justification by faith as wrought by personal conversion and a life of good works as its appropriate fruit. Amongst the most influential were: Charles Simeon of Cambridge (1759–1836) whose earnest preaching persuaded many generations of university students to enter the ordained

10. Tindal, *Christianity as Old as the Creation.*

ministry; William Wilberforce (1759–1833), who led the battle in Parliament to abolition slavery in the British Empire; and Anthony Ashley Cooper, Earl of Shaftesbury (1801–85), who fought to improve the working and living conditions of the poor.

The *High Church Oxford Movement* produced *Tracts for the Times*, a series of publications that called the Church of England to recover its spiritual heritage as an ancient catholic institution as described and defended by the Caroline divines in the Seventeenth Century. In his contributions John Henry Newman argued that the Church of England was a *via media*, following the beliefs and practices of the early church uncorrupted either by papalism or Protestantism. In fact, Newman was the first person to coin the term "Anglicanism" as a separate branch of Christendom. Although he eventually found his own arguments unconvincing and converted to Roman Catholicism, other early Tractarians such as John Keble and E.B. Pusey remained. Using their immense scholarship, they continued to promote the Oxford Movement's vision of Anglo-Catholicism, which in the Twentieth Century would succeed in reshaping the liturgy and, indeed, the very self-understanding of much of Anglicanism.

Finally, *the Broad Church movement* responded to the advent of German biblical criticism and Darwin's theory of evolution by drawing on the Eighteenth Century's commitment to the primacy of reason in theological discourse. Listen to Benjamin Jowett in his chapter "On the Interpretation of Scripture" in the landmark book *Essays and Reviews* (1860):

> Almost all intelligent persons are agreed that the earth has existed for myriads of ages; the best informed are of opinion that the history of nations extends back some thousand years before the Mosaic chronology; recent discoveries in geology may perhaps open a further vista of existence for the human species, while it is possible, and may one day be known, that mankind spread not from one but from many centres over the globe; or as others say, that the supply of links which are at present wanting in the chain of animal life may lead to new conclusions respecting the origin of man.

And:

> [T]he time has come when it is no longer possible to ignore the results of criticism, it is of importance that Christianity should be seen to be in harmony with them . . . It is a mischief that critical observations which any intelligent man can make for himself, should be ascribed to atheism or unbelief. It would be a strange

and almost incredible thing that the Gospel, which at first made war only on the vices of mankind, should now be opposed to one of the highest and rarest of human virtues—the love of truth. And that in the present day the great object of Christianity should be, not to change the lives of men, but to prevent them from changing their opinions; that would be a singular inversion of the purposes for which Christ came into the world. The Christian religion is in a false position when all the tendencies of knowledge are opposed to it. Such a position cannot be long maintained, or can only end in the withdrawal of the educated classes from the influences of religion.

What remains may be comprised in a few precepts, or rather is the expansion of a single one. *Interpret the Scripture like any other book.* [11]

Note the essentially moralist nature of Jowett's argument. The purpose of Christianity is to inculcate virtues, not specific doctrinal beliefs. When received, theological convictions conflict with the advances of science, the power of religion to encourage morality is in danger of being lost. We must adjust our religious persuasions to what intelligent people can give assent in good conscience.

The influence of the Victorian commitment to morality did not end with merely shaping the broad church movement's justification for adherence to reason. The vibrant presence of three different understandings of Anglicanism at the same time presented a national church with a significant crisis of self-understanding. If neither a common doctrinal understanding nor even a common set of worship practices held the Church of England together, what could? In the end, Victorian moralism afforded a way forward. Since each different stream of Anglicanism still emphasised the necessity of repentance and ethical renewal, all could agree that what ultimately mattered was the common end of a better people, even if they could not agree as to a common theological means to do so.

## *Fifth Phase of Anglicanism:*
## *The Current Situation*

During the Twentieth Century, the British Empire gradually receded, leaving behind an increasing number of independent national churches. From these relics of empire grew a vibrant, global fellowship of thirty-eight

11. Jowett, "On the Interpretation of Scripture," 383–84, 412, 416.

autonomous provinces knitted together as fellow heirs to the Anglican tradition. At first, the emerging Anglican Communion seemed to develop into
a worldwide ecclesiastical family, united by a common understanding of
the essentials of Christian faith and practice, but expressing them in faithful ways appropriate for each national church's own cultural context. However, as the century progressed, materially affluent western society became
increasingly secular, rendering public morality less rooted in theological
convictions and more and more a matter of civil and then simple human
rights. As a result, in addition to the intellectual moralists who directly descended from *Essays and Reviews*, a growing number of "open" Evangelicals
and "affirming" Anglo-Catholics championed the primacy of reason over
Scripture and Tradition. So much so, that by the beginning of the Twenty-
First Century, the fault lines within Anglicanism were no longer principally
between the low, high and broad church parties. Rather, the main division
had become between those Anglicans committed to a secular-justice-driv-
en redemption of human society and those Evangelicals, Anglo-Catholics
and now Charismatics as well who still saw the first task of the church as
to proclaim the atoning sacrifice of Christ on the cross as the basis for humanity's reconciliation with God as well as one another. At the beginning
of the Twenty-First Century, we are witnessing the slow transition of the
Anglican Communion as an ecclesial community united by basic theological and moral convictions to a community of mutual conversation about
the disparate convictions of its member provinces.

Thus, in the light of the divergent nature of its development, we will
have to concede that today there is no such thing as "*the* Anglican Way," but
rather "Anglican *ways*." Hence, to answer our second question—"Is there
anything distinctive about Anglicanism's approach to Christianity?"—we
will have to begin by examining the three historic streams. Yet, even this
approach would seem initially less than promising, since, in fact, each Anglican church party began by denying its distinctiveness.

Reformation Anglicanism saw itself as part of a broad reformed theological movement to restore ancient Christianity to its Scriptural practices.
In fact, under Edward VI, Thomas Cranmer worked very hard to convene a
Protestant version of the Council of Trent so as to create a common confession of belief, although to no effect. Caroline Anglo-Catholicism presented
itself as simply repristinating the undivided church. Even the Modernist,
reason-led Anglicanism that arose out of the Enlightenment argued that
its tenets merely pointed to the simple truths of Nature. To paraphrase the

English Deist Mathew Tindale, rather than seeing itself as something distinctive, Modernist Anglicanism sees itself as old as the Creation.

Yet, despite this typical English reticence to put themselves forward, at least one form of Anglicanism did indeed develop a distinctive vision of the human life that formed its understanding of liberal learning. Let's take a closer look at the first Anglican self-understanding, Cranmer's vision for the Church of England as outlined in the sixteenth-century formularies.

## Part II: The Uniqueness of Reformation Anglicanism

Based on the novel by Nicholas Sparks, *The Notebook* is a romantic film about a wonderfully obsessive love.[12] The plot starts off with an old man in a nursing home reading a story from an old battered notebook to an equally elderly woman each day. At first she is hesitate to be with this stranger, no matter how kind. However, as he begins to read through the story of young working-class Noah Calhoun and his doggedly enduring pursuit of the privileged but sweet Allie Nelson, she is initially intrigued, then enthralled and always asks him to go on. The notebook's narrative charts the ups and downs of Allie and Noah's courtship, his initial daredevil stunt on a Ferris wheel to get her attention, their growing utter joy in being in each other's company, their incredibly painful estrangement because of parental shenanigans and the difficult obstacles that had to be overcome before their eventual reunion, leading finally to their marriage and wonderful life together. Gradually, as time goes on, it becomes increasingly clear that the notebook is the elderly woman's own story about their story, her life with the elderly man reading to her, a story she herself wrote down in that very notebook but cannot now remember because of her Alzheimer's. That is why the old man is reading it to her with such tender, doggedly enduring devotion and love.

Eventually, the moment comes for which Noah has been waiting. Allie's eyes are opened, and she says, 'How long do we have?' Noah replies, 'We had five minutes last time.' 'I want to dance. Hold me close once again,' Allie asks. Noah takes her in his arms, and they slowly dance—the very picture of recovery of self at last, of finally coming home again, of inner peace finally found, of a long journey finally completed. But after of few splendid minutes of mutual rapture, enjoying the utter joy of once again mutually knowing one another's company, Allie cries out, 'Who is this

12. Sparks, *The Notebook*.

stranger grabbing me?' Noah bites his finger in angst. Paradise regained only to be lost again.

What a wonderful allegory of the human condition in general! Deceived by the foggy lies of human nature's millennia-long struggle with spiritual Alzheimer's, we find ourselves driven to push away from our Creator and his life-giving love, the One in whose arms alone we finally feel at home. Only the direct, on-going intervention of his heavenly wooing has the power periodically to break through our confused haze. By telling us once again the story of his dogged pursuit of a relationship with us, he calls forth from deep within us the recognition that his story is our story and so restores us to our true selves in his loving embrace. Here is the heart of liberal learning for the Reformation Anglicanism.

As we have seen, Modernist Anglicanism wishes to interpret the Bible as a book just like any other book. Nothing could be further from the world of the English Reformers. Deeply influenced by Erasmus' rhetorical theology, they saw Scripture not only as God's unique revelation of the truth that saves but also as his unique instrument to turn their hearts to embrace and embody those truths:

> The words of holy Scripture be called *words of everlasting life*; for they be God's instrument, ordained for the same purpose. They have power to converteth through God's promise, and they be effectual through God's assistance; and, being received in a faithful heart, they have ever an heavenly spiritual working in them.[13]

For those who would "ruminate and as it were chew the cud" of Scripture, God worked through the regular repetition of biblical truths to engraft in them not only saving faith but also a steadfastness in the pursuit of personal holiness that would gradually transform their character to mirror what they were reading:

> And there is nothing that so much establisheth our faith and trust in God, that so much conserveth innocency and pureness of the heart, and also of outward godly life and conversation, as continual reading and meditation of God's word. For that thing which, by perpetual use of reading of holy Scripture and diligent searching of the same, is deeply printed and graven in the heart, at length turneth almost into nature.[14]

13. Griffiths, ed., *Two Books of Homilies*, 9.

14. Ibid., 10, 15.

In short, the spiritual effect of God's supernatural agency through Scripture was the on-going reorientation of a believer's heart:

> This word whosoever is diligent to read, and in his heart to print that he readeth, the great affection to the transitory things of this world shall be minished in him, and the great desire of heavenly things, that be therein promised of God, shall increase in him.[15]

Hence, "*the hearing and keeping of* [Scripture] maketh us *blessed, sanctifieth* us and maketh us holy." Little wonder, then, the "Homily on Scripture" urged that "[t]hese books therefore ought to be much in our hands, in our eyes, in our ears, in our mouths, but most of all in our hearts."[16]

This supernatural redirection of human affections through the liberal learning of Scripture lay at the very heart of Cranmer's understanding of the Christian life. In his *Loci communes* (1521), Philip Melanchthon had argued that the affections of the heart determined the choices of the will. Hence, after the Fall, both human reason and the will were held captive by the affection of self-love, i.e., the concupiscence of the flesh. Therefore, moral transformation could come about only through the intervention of an outside force, the Holy Spirit. When the good news of justification by faith was proclaimed, the Spirit, working through God's Word, assured believers of their salvation. This new confidence in God's gracious goodwill towards them reoriented their affections, calming their turbulent hearts and inflaming in them a grateful love in return. These new godly affections would continually have to fight to restrain the ever-present stirrings of the concupiscence of the flesh. Nevertheless, because of the renewing work of the Holy Spirit believers now had the necessary desire and ability to live a life of deepening repentance.[17]

For Cranmer, the Lutheran assurance of salvation was the long sought missing key to unlock societal transformation. In his mature view, fear, shame, guilt and duty did not have the power to stop people from sinning, only a love for God was stronger than the pull of sin. And, according to Scripture, the power to love God can only come from first being loved by him. Therefore, only the promise of free salvation made possible by God's love could inspire grateful human love in response.

15. Ibid., 9–10.

16. Ibid., 9.

17. Null, *Thomas Cranmer's Doctrine of Repentance*, 98–102.

In comments to Henry VIII in January 1538, Cranmer explained how the biblical promise of assured salvation in Christ was the key to drawing believers away from self-gratification towards the grateful service of their Savior:

> But, if the profession of our faith of the remission of our own sins enter within us into the deepness of our hearts, then it must kindle a warm fire of love in our hearts towards God, and towards all others for the love of God,—a fervent mind to seek and procure God's honour, will, and pleasure in all things,—a good will and mind to help every man and to do good unto them, so far as our might, wisdom, learning, counsel, health, strength, and all other gifts which we have received of God, will extend,—and, *in summa*, a firm intent and purpose to do all that is good, and leave all that is evil.[18]

Cranmer incorporated this teaching into his "Homily on Salvation"—the normative Anglican explanation of justification according to Article 11 of the Thirty-Nine Articles: "For the right and true christian faith is . . . to have a sure trust and confidence in God's merciful promises, to be saved from everlasting damnation by Christ: whereof doth follow a loving heart to obey his commandments."[19] When the benefits of God's merciful grace were considered, unless they were "desperate persons" with "hearts harder than stones," people would be moved to give themselves wholly unto God and the service of their neighbors.[20] In short, for Cranmer grace produced gratitude. Gratitude birthed love. Love led to repentance. Repentance brought about good works, and good works contributed to a better society.

## *The Two Feedings on Christ*

Cranmer went on to argue that this essential renewal of human affections came by feeding on the scriptural promises in two forms. The first way happens whenever Christians "record in their minds the beneficial death of our Saviour Christ, chewing it by faith in the cud of their spirit, and digesting it in their hearts, feeding and comforting themselves with that heavenly meat, although they daily receive not the sacrament thereof."[21] The turning

18. Cox, *Writings and Disputations of Thomas Cranme,r* 86.

19. Ibid., 133

20. Ibid., 134.

21. Cox, *Cranmer*, 70–71.

side of the Bible meant that believers could experience spiritual union with the risen Lord at any time and in any place through encountering him in Scripture.

Nevertheless, Cranmer also acknowledged and encouraged another means of feeding on biblical truth, Holy Communion. "Christ ordained the sacrament of his body and blood in bread and wine to preach unto us" through

> sensible signs and tokens whereby to allure and to draw us to more strength and more constant faith in him. So that the eating and drinking of this sacramental bread and wine is, as it were, show-ing of Christ before our eyes, a smelling of him with our noses, feeling and groping of him with our hands, and an eating, chew-ing, digesting, and feeding upon him to our spiritual strength and perfection.[22]

In other words, Cranmer believed that Almighty God understood that human learning happened best through experiences that involved as many of our senses as possible. Consequently, Jesus had instituted the sacramen-tal preaching of Holy Communion so as to use all of our senses—touch, taste, sight and smell as well as hearing, so as to enable "feeding in Christ's promises."[23] Therefore, the sacrament was an even more effective way for believers to have their "spiritual feeding increased," enabling them to "grow and wax continually more strong in Christ, until at the last they shall come to the full measure and perfection in Christ."[24]

To foster these two feedings on Christ's promises, Cranmer refash-ioned the rhythms of the Anglican liturgical life. On Sundays, the celebra-tion of the sacrament was retained as the principle worship service, but it was so re-ordered as to begin with a liturgy of the Word to inspire spiritual feeding first and only then moved forward to provide a sacramental feeding. However, Cranmer made an even greater break with the medieval past when it came to week-day parish worship. He replaced the traditional round of votive masses with Scripture-based services of prayer derived from the mo-nastic tradition. Simplifying the ancient Benedictine pattern of seven-fold daily offices to merely two, Cranmer instituted Morning and Evening Prayer as the pattern of daily worship for all members of the parish. Although the prayers for Morning and Evening Prayer were thoroughly imbued with the

22. Ibid., 41–42.
23. Ibid., 71
24. Ibid.

words of Scripture, at the very heart of the new services was the restoration of the ancient church practice of reading through the Bible itself each year. As a result, according to the Daily Office Lectionary in Cranmer's prayer book the whole Psalter was recited every month, the New Testament was read three times a year (except for the Book of Revelation) and most of the Old Testament once a year. As the Preface to the prayer book expressed it, the hope was that "the people (by daily hearing of holy scripture read in the Church) should continually profit more and more in the knowledge of God, and be the more inflamed with the love of his true religion."[25] At last the Anglican Church had services which enabled the English people to fulfil Cranmer's exhortation in the "Homily on Scripture" "*night and day*" to "muse and *have meditation* and contemplation in" the Bible.[26]

## Scripture and Ceremonies

Despite all Cranmer's attempts in his second prayer book of 1552 to provide a clear presentation of Protestant teaching, not all Reformed theologians were happy with the result. In particular, John Knox, then a chaplain to Edward VI, felt that not all ungodly ceremonies of church tradition had yet been eliminated. He strenuously objected that continuing to kneel to receive Communion was an act of idolatry. He demanded that communicants sit instead, since "it is not commanded in the Scripture to kneel, and whatsoever is not commanded in the Scripture, is against the Scripture and utterly unlawful and ungodly."[27] In other words, for Knox and his followers, everything a person did in every aspect of life had to have a clear biblical command or rule. Otherwise, it did not proceed from faith and, thus, was sin (Romans 14:23). And what was true of individuals was, of course, especially true for the church. Historians call this idea that every worship practice must be grounded in a clear biblical commandment the *regulative principle*.

Cranmer, however, categorically rejected the idea that liturgical ceremonies were "to be esteemed equal with God's law."[28] He made a decisive distinction between unalterable saving truth, divinely revealed in Jesus Christ and faithfully recorded in Scripture alone, and changing human

25. Ketley, *The Two Liturgies*, 17.

26. Griffiths, *Two Books of Homilies*, 15.

27. Dairmaid MacCulloch, *Thomas Cranmer: A Life*, 525–29.

28. Ketley, *Two Liturgies*, 157.

traditions of the church by which the divinely established gospel message was expressed and conveyed to successive generations of Christians. The essentials of salvation, that is, matters of faith and morals, had to be founded on divine authority and, therefore, on the Word of God alone—nothing in addition to it and nothing contrary to it. Rites and ceremonies, however, as particular expressions of the Gospel for different eras and cultures, were derived from the institutional authority of the church. They must merely not contradict Scripture. The church could use or adapt other sources, like ancient traditions such as monasticism, or it could institute new liturgies more in keeping with contemporary needs, even if such practices were not explicitly detailed in Scripture. Cranmer's distinction lies behind that famous Anglican dictum "Holy Scripture contains all things necessary for salvation," namely, the Bible reveals everything needed for establishing saving beliefs and faithful morality (regulative on doctrine), but not a blueprint for everything in life (normative on everything else).[29]

In essence, Knox believed that the only truly authentic human culture was found within the pages of Scripture which the church was called to manifest in the world. For Cranmer, ever the humanist, such thinking simply attempted to sacrifice the creative diversity and historic development of human cultures on a Procrustean bed of false biblical authority. He considered the Gospel message to be godly leaven able to transform the unique culture of every nation. Cranmer won the argument with the council by the donnish quip that if Knox really wanted the Church of England to receive Communion in the biblical manner, they would need to recline on the ground in the chancel rather than sit at a table. While seeming perhaps merely a witty retort *ad absurdum*, Cranmer was actually pointing out that there was no such thing as only one "biblical" way to eat food. The manner of one's eating was a thing indifferent, determined by one's cultural background. The later famous dispute between Knox and Richard Cox in Frankfurt during the Marian Exile conveniently summarizes the difference in the Knoxian and Cranmerian approach to church and culture. Cox insisted on using Cranmer's liturgy so as to "have the face off an English church in exile." Knox, however, wanted a purer worship service which would have "the face of Christ's church."[30]

29. This principle is first mentioned in the "Homily on Scripture" in the *Book of Homilies* and attributed to Chrysostom (Griffiths, *Two Books of Homilies*, 8). The tenet reappears again in the *Ordinal* (Ketley, *Two Liturgies*, 177, 183) and then finally in the *Articles of Religion* (Hardwick, *History of the Articles of Religion*, 294).

30. *Troubles at Frankfort*, 37–59, especially 38, 49 and 59; Laing, *Works of Knox IV*,

In the end, the 1552 prayer book retained kneeling to receive Communion, and Knox had to be content with the last-minute 'Black Rubric' which specifically denied a papist interpretation of the practice. The following year Cranmer sealed his victory by including his understanding of ceremonies in the *Articles of Religion*:

> It is not necessary that traditions and ceremonies be in all places one, or utterly like. For at all times they have been diverse, and may be changed according to the diversity of countries and men's manners, so that nothing be ordained against God's Word.[31]

This article would become the historic basis for the Anglican Communion, namely, a worldwide fellowship of individual ecclesial provinces who shared a received understanding of Scripture's revelation of saving faith and morals but who remained free to express this common doctrinal inheritance in culturally appropriate ways for their own era and societies. No doubt Cranmer was concerned that Knox's approach would not only lead to Christians looking at Scripture primarily as a book of rules—something which was anathema to Cranmer's promotion of affective biblical reading—but also eventually render the church and ever-evolving human cultures deaf to one another, greatly impeding the church's global mission.

## Part III: Liberal Learning in Reformation Anglicanism

Thus, for Reformation Anglicanism, the Bible was the sole source for salvation. Scripture told people both the truth about themselves so they could grasp their need for God as well as his plan of redemption so they could recognize his saving work in their lives. The church, either by relying on tradition or reason or both, still had no authority to add to or subtract from the Bible's unchanging message of salvation. Yet the Bible did more than merely tell people what they need to know to be saved. God's Word was also the very instrument through which his Holy Spirit went forth to bring about the salvation of his people. Just like with human speech, with God's words went forth his Ruach, his life-giving breathe. As the promises of Scripture were proclaimed through preaching and the sacraments, the Holy Spirit wrote God's very own words on the hearts of his people, awakening in them saving trust in God's plan of redemption and alluring their

41–49, 55–57 (spelling modernized).

31. Hardwick, *History of the Articles,* 318 (spelling modernized).

wayward wills to begin to love God and their neighbors as a response to his unconditional love for them. Therefore, promoting the Bible was the number one priority for the English reformers.

Nevertheless, as indispensable as Scripture was for human flourishing, God's Word contained no detailed blueprint for how to proclaim its immutable truths aptly to ever-evolving individual cultures and eras. God had to guide his people afresh in mission for each generation. For this specific task, both tradition and reason became essential, if still secondary, contributors to the fullness of human life and liberal learning. For Cranmer, church tradition was the record of how Christians through the centuries had sought to inculcate Scripture's saving faith and morals into the social and ecclesial institutions of each era and culture. Because gospel inculturation is always more of an art than a science, Cranmer saw the successes and failures of the past as helpful guides for leaders of the contemporary church in their own quest to express Christian truth both faithfully and effectively in the fabric of their society. Tradition that withstood the plumb-line test of Scripture served as the treasury of the collective memory of Christian wisdom on living out the Gospel in a fallen world.

Yet, the divine wisdom of Scripture, even as aided by the human wisdom of the Christians who have sought to live out its message in their day, still had to be applied to the current and future needs of the church, its members and its mission. Of course, by definition the application of Christian wisdom required comparison—comparisons between different parts of Scripture to establish an exegesis, then comparisons between this exegesis and earlier Christian commentators to be sure of its soundness, finally comparisons between this exegesis and past as well as present Christian practice in order to determine the best norms for current society. Of course, deduction through comparison, by its very nature requires reason, and in theological matters, reason as aided the Holy Spirit working through his Word. Reformation Anglicanism did not somehow leap ahead two centuries and advocate some sort of Enlightenment concept of autonomous reason. Not only is such a thing historically anachronistic, but the Reformers rejected the scholasticism of their day precisely because they felt it relied too heavily on even graced-aided reason in doctrinal matters which they reserved for divine revelation alone. As a faithfully exponent of Cranmer's theological legacy, Richard Hooker made clear that his "theological reason" was derived from comparing Scripture to itself and then applying these truths to his society.[32]

We can see Reformation Anglicanism's three-string cord for Christian wisdom at work in Cranmer's liturgical projects, perhaps the very thing most other Protestants see as distinctively Anglican. Cranmer was particularly clear that when the devotional practices of previous generations continued to further the biblical message in the current culture, these should be honoured and maintained. Those which failed to do so, however, were to be modified in the light of God's Word and contemporary needs or stricken altogether. The richness of Anglican liturgy was the direct result. Despite the beauty of the historic Latin liturgy, Cranmer's prayer books were in English so as to meet the contemporary missional needs of its society. The words themselves were stitched together from Scripture into patterns carefully polished by centuries of human praxis so as to proclaim in word and sacrament the timeless biblical message for sixteenth-century England. In short, Cranmer's prayer books were both reformed and catholic, ancient and universal in its gospel message, yet simultaneously accommodated to its specific culture and era.

Now at last we can summarize the distinctives of Reformation Anglicanism's understanding of human life and liberal learning:

1. The heart of the Christian life is a renewal of the affections made possible by feeding supernaturally on the promises of Scripture.

2. The heart of this on-going process of renewal is Christian worship. Like the early church, Cranmer wanted Anglican liturgy to tell over and over again the old, old story through its verbal proclamation in preaching and in its visible retelling in the sacraments until every Christian in England found his or her own place in that story.

3. The telling side of Scripture should never be permitted to overshadow its turning side. The power of what God has promised to do in, through and for us should never be vitiated by an over-preoccupation

---

32. "Not meaning thereby mine own reason as now it is reported, but true, sound, divine reason; reason whereby those conclusions might be out of St. Paul demonstrated, and not probably discoursed only, reason proper to that science whereby the things of God are known; which out of the principles in Scripture that are plain, soundly deducteth more doubtful inferences, in such sort that being heard they neither can be denied, nor any thing repugnant unto them received, but whatsoever was before otherwise by miscollecting gathered out of darker places, is thereby forced to yield itself, and the true consonant meaning of sentences not understood is brought to light," Keble, ed., *The Works of Mr. Richard Hooker*, 3:594–95.

of what we are called to do to please God. We seek to become more like God, not so that he will love us more, but precisely because he has already lavished on us more love than we can ever comprehend.

4. Church tradition and human reason have a vital, if specifically secondary, role to play in cultivating the Christian wisdom necessary for the flourishing of the church's mission and its members in our time.

5. As we regularly honour God by telling his story, we discover afresh how his love honours us in ways we could never have imagined. Consequently, our minds are renewed, our hearts inflamed and our wills empowered so that we, too, in our day, can add a further chapter to God's glorious notebook of his love story with humanity. Thanks be to God.

# Bibliography

Cox, J. E. *Writings and Disputations of Thomas Cranmer, Archbishop of Canterbury, Martyr, 1556, Relative to the Sacrament of the Lord's Supper*. Cambridge: Parker Society, 1864.

Foxe, John. *Actes and Monuments*. http://www.johnfoxe.org.

Griffiths, John. *The Two Books of Homilies Appointed to be Read in Churches*. Oxford: Oxford University Press, 1864.

Hardwick, Charles. *History of the Articles*. London: Bell & Daldy, 1859.

Hill, W. Speed, et al. *The Folger Library Edition of The Works of Richard Hooker*. Cambridge: Belknap Press, Harvard University Press, 1977–1990.

Jowett, Benjamin. "On the Interpretation of Scripture" in *Essays and Reviews*, section 3 (1860) 137–51.

Ketley, Joseph. *The Two Liturgies, A.D. 1549, and A.D. 1552: with other Documents set forth by Authority in the reign of King Edward VI*. Cambridge: The Parker Society/Cambridge University Press, 1864.

MacCulloch, Dairmaid. *Thomas Cranmer: A Life*. New Haven: Yale University Press, 1998.

Null, Ashley. "Official Tudor Homilies." In *Oxford Handbook of the Early Modern Sermon*, edited by Hugh Adlington, Peter McCullough, and Emma Rhatigan, 348–65. Oxford: Oxford University Press, 2011.

———. "Princely Marital Problems and the Reformers' Solutions." In *Sister Reformations: England and the German Empire in the Sixteenth Century*, edited by Dorothea Wendebourg. Tübingen: Mohr Siebeck, forthcoming.

———. *Thomas Cranmer's Doctrine of Repentance: Renewing the Power to Love*. Oxford: Oxford University Press, 2000.

Quantin, Jean-Louis. *The Church of England and Christian Antiquity: The Construction of a Confessional Identity in the 17th Century*. Oxford: Oxford University Press, 2009.

Sparks, Nicholas. *The Notebook*. New York: Warner, 1996.

Tindal, Matthew. *Christianity as Old as the Creation; or, the Gospel a Republication of the Religion of Nature.* London: n.p., 1730.

Wallace, Dewey D. Jr. *"Via Media? A Paradigm Shift." Anglican and Episcopal History* 72 (March 2003) 2–21.

# A Mennonite View of Life and Learning:
## Practicing the Way of Jesus

*Sara Wenger Shenk*

A FEW YEARS AGO, Jewish ethicist and educator, Hanan Alexander, published a book called *Reclaiming Goodness—Education and the Spiritual Quest.* He asserts that "people are searching for spirituality today . . . because comprehensive visions of the good are conspicuously absent from modern culture." Alexander further states that "education is not first and foremost about acquiring knowledge, or gaining identity, or insuring group continuity . . . but rather about empowering a person to choose a vision of the good life."[1]

## A Vision of the Good Life

What might a vision of the good life look like, I wonder? My mind quickly goes to Micah 4:3–4. We used to sing it this way:

> Everyone 'neath a vine and fig tree, shall live in peace and unafraid.

> And into plowshares turn their swords; they shall learn of war no more.

Another vision of the good life appears in Acts 2:43–47 (NRSV):

> Awe came upon everyone, because many wonders and signs were being done by the apostles. All who believed were together and had all things in common; they would sell their possessions and goods and distribute the proceeds to all, as any had need. Day by

---

1. Alexander, *Reclaiming Goodness,* 9.

day, as they spent much time together in the temple, they broke bread at home and ate their food with glad and generous hearts, praising God and having the goodwill of all the people. And day by day the Lord added to their number those who were being saved.

The Bible provides us with many powerful and compelling visions of the good life. There are all kinds of ways these visions become lodged in our consciousness. How do we educate for a distinctive and vibrant vision of the good life, with all it entails about living at peace with self, God, neighbor and creation? And what might that look like within a Mennonite vision for life and learning? These are the questions that guide my reflection below.

A story comes to mind that may help to set a framework. Dr. Vincent Harding was a recent guest at Anabaptist Mennonite Biblical Seminary (AMBS), where I serve as president. He was a longtime friend and co-worker of Dr. Martin Luther King Jr. He made a comment that captured my imagination about "organizing goodness." But first some background, in a story that is recounted in more detail in *Widening the Circle: Experiments in Christian Discipleship* edited by Joanna Shenk.

Harding had been involved in an "experimental" biracial congregation in the late 1950s and 1960s called Woodlawn Mennonite Church in Chicago. The congregation chose to have one white pastor and one African American pastor, a radical move at that time.

At one point, Harding travelled along with two other black men and two white men from the congregation of Woodlawn Mennonite Church on an outreach trip through the deep South (so the story is told). After passing through Arkansas and Mississippi into Alabama, Harding suggested that they call on King, who was working at Ebenezer Baptist Church in Atlanta. King was recuperating from stab wounds suffered on a visit to Harlem, but his wife, Coretta, invited the group to visit and to see if King was interested in talking to these guests. King received the five men in his bathrobe and pajamas, Harding recalled. "He had a tremendous sense of humor," Harding said. "He could not stop kidding us about how we had made it through Mississippi alive."

Harding and his wife, Rosemarie decided to move to Atlanta in 1961, "right around the corner from the Kings," to aid in the civil rights struggle as part of a Mennonite group. They had a close association for at least ten years. Harding occasionally drafted speeches for Martin Luther King, including King's famous anti-Vietnam speech, "A Time to Break Silence," which King delivered on April 4, 1967 at Riverside Church in New York City, exactly a year before he was assassinated.

Harding said at the recent event at AMBS, "Martin used to love to say this: 'We've got to organize goodness.'" And Harding asked: "What would it mean to organize goodness? Is that what seminaries are for?"

My mind has not stopped spinning around this intriguing question ever since. I recognized immediately that it named what I believe to be AMBS's mission as a learning community: to educate leaders for God's reconciling mission in the world. As a seminary, we are called to educate leaders who are prepared to form and guide communities of shalom; communities where goodness is allowed to thrive.

What does it mean to organize goodness? How is it organized at Templeton Honors College? In your family? In your congregation? In the neighborhoods of Philadelphia? In our nation? Philosophers from Socrates and Aristotle onward have debated what it means to be good and what the good life entails. Our Scriptures tell us that God organized goodness out of chaos. God looked at all that was created and proclaimed it very good.

The goodness of God. Being good. The good life. There are no end of ways to ponder what goodness looks like and how we are called to "organize goodness."

Each of our traditions has stewarded particular gifts. The tradition I was raised within is primarily Mennonite; more commonly referred to as Anabaptist. The Anabaptist movement is often called the radical wing of the sixteenth-century Reformation. The Anabaptist movement gave rise to several denominations, one of which is Mennonite. As a movement, it seems to be experiencing a renewal of interest in a large wave of so-called new Anabaptists in our day from many denominations and backgrounds.

Living with appreciation over many years for the strengths of my tradition leads me to ask these questions: (1) What would it look like to embrace a "comprehensive vision of the good" inspired by Jesus' Sermon on the Mount? (2) What would the character of our communities be if we truly believed that the good news of Christ's peace is central to God's grand and good mission for the world? (3) What if we pursued an expression of Christianity in which every day we sought to follow Jesus by daily discipleship? (4) What if we sought to give shape to a vision for God's shalom by organizing goodness (if you will) in the social practices of our community life?

A key theme implied by the above questions is that the good news of Jesus Christ—the Gospel—is not an abstract concept so much as a comprehensive vision of goodness made real in daily life; made real in how we live together; in how we become the grace-filled body of Christ in the world.

## Anabaptist Perspectives on Life and Learning

In my book, *Anabaptist Ways of Knowing: A Conversation about Tradition-Based Critical Education,* I discuss a classic Anabaptist affirmation stated by Hans Denck, an early Anabaptist leader which reads, "No one can truly know [Christ] unless he follow him in life, and no one may follow him unless he has first known him." Mennonite historian, Irvin B. Horst, described this as an epistemological principle and a distinctive emphasis within the sixteenth century on the nature and method of knowing.[2]

For the Anabaptists, neither church structures nor doctrines were considered as centrally important as modeling one's life on Jesus. It was in practicing the way of Jesus, by following Jesus in daily life, that true faith manifested itself. And the Anabaptists emphasized how important it was to do this not only as individuals, but as entire communities who seek to model in their life together the early followers of Jesus. They believed that only by living into the practices of Jesus as individuals and as communities, they would come to understand God and God's will for how we are to live.

I want to name in broad strokes, three characteristics of the Anabaptist movement that inform a Mennonite view of life and learning. This is an approach to organizing goodness that Mennonites have stewarded. I discuss them in more depth in *Anabaptist Ways of Knowing.*

## Discipleship: Patterning Our Lives on Jesus Christ

For the Anabaptists, the life, teachings, and cross of Jesus Christ constituted the normative pattern for shaping their life in the world. This concept has far ranging educational implications. What does it mean to identify so closely with someone that one's life is shaped by that life? What does it mean to "indwell" the Jesus story bodily, embodying that story in ways that transform one's life and spirit? And how would one go about that?

2. See Irwin B. Horst, Proposition V of Theses, appended to his doctoral dissertation for its defense, cited by Swartley in "The Anabaptists Use of Scripture: Contemporary Applications and Prospects," *Anabaptist Currents,* edited by Bowman and Longenecker, 70.

Well clearly, it would be by spending a lot of time with the story of Jesus, which is found in Scripture. It is very evident from their writings that the Anabaptists formed much of their thinking and speaking from the Scriptures. Their immersion in Scripture grew out of their desire to live faithful lives of discipleship. To know the Scriptures so well that they were formed by the language, metaphors, practices and vision of Scripture was an all-consuming passion for the Anabaptists.

By "abiding in Christ" and with the transformative power of the Holy Spirit, many of the Anabaptists were able to renounce violence despite incredible persecution. They were able to share material and spiritual resources in their exercise of mutual care and communal discipline.

What would it mean in our day, I wonder, to be so immersed in Scripture (above all the Jesus story) that it becomes the primary shaper of our vision of the good, and our daily practices?

## Hermeneutical Community: Discerning Truth Communally

The Anabaptists' immersion in Scripture grew out of their desire to live faithful lives of discipleship. They were committed to reading Scripture together communally, believing that the Holy Spirit would empower them to discern truth and faithful ways to practice that truth.

Stuart Murray, author of a popular book called *The Naked Anabaptist* wrote in his doctoral thesis entitled "Spirit, Discipleship, Community: The Contemporary Significance of Anabaptist Hermeneutics" that designating the local congregation as the "locus of interpretation" was arguably the most important and distinctive Anabaptist contribution to sixteenth-century biblical interpretation. Within the context of community, every believer is empowered to offer a perspective. And everyone together relies on the presence of the Holy Spirit.

A community, a congregation of believers meeting together around Scripture in order to discern how to live as disciples, how to organize goodness, has educational implications. The Anabaptist model of an interpreting community is an enormously significant contribution by Mennonites to a vision for life and learning.

## Ecclesiology: Community for Transformation

The Anabaptists believed that the church is called to be a pioneering, model-building community of God's people in the larger society. Their understanding was that the church is to be distinct from the world as a conscience, and servant within the world, embodying Jesus' sacrificial love and love of enemy.

The Anabaptists provided a critique of and dissent from any form of Constantinian or establishment Christendom that did not involve voluntary commitment in defining a visible community. John Howard Yoder, well known Mennonite theologian, suggests that the primary social structure through which the gospel works to change other structures is the Christian community, the Christian church. The calling of the church, he said, is to be "the conscience and the servant within human society."[3]

Richard Hays agrees that the church has a "modeling mission" to embody an "alternative order that anticipates God's will for the reconciliation of the world."[4] The educational implications of this seem to point toward a practical way of knowing—a way of knowing that is centered in the practices of the faith community, practices that are meant to organize goodness.

## Practical Roots of Knowledge

Persons from a variety of disciplines have taken increased interest in the function of practices in our "knowing." Craig Dykstra and Dorothy Bass have written extensively about the function of shared practices in communities. They describe practices as shared activities through which persons come to know and through which perspectives on reality are formed. They are sites of learning that join ethical and epistemological dimensions. They have been referred to as embodied thought.

I referred to Hans Denck, the early Anabaptist leader, above. He said, "No one can truly know [Christ] unless he follow him in life, and no one may follow him unless he has first known him."[5] As an epistemological principle, this seems to suggest that rather than truth about God or about Christ being regarded as a disembodied, abstract concept, it is more helpful, particularly from an Anabaptist perspective, to think of truth as deriv-

3. Yoder, *The Politics of Jesus*, 155.

4. Hays, *The Moral Vision*, 253

5. Cited in Klassen, *Anabaptism in Outline*, 87.

ing from the concrete practices of daily life. We will know the truth only by following Jesus in the concrete practices of healing, liberation, and justice.

Rather than first establishing the truthfulness of the Scriptures based on historical criticism or textual analysis, a practical approach to knowledge suggests that it is in practicing the Gospel that we become able to interpret it properly—and to know its goodness.

Pedagogy has often tended to focus on conveying information. Concentrating on the bodiliness of practices allows us to think about education in more holistic ways. An educational approach that focuses on practices will allow a fuller range of forms of knowing. Practical approaches to knowing will pay attention to such experiential elements as images, rituals, habits, cycles, routines, and daily rhythms.

Social Scientist, Paul Connerton, in his book, *How Societies Remember*, argues that bodily social memory is an essential aspect of social memory that has previously been badly neglected. In fact, he says that every group will entrust to bodily automatisms the values they are most anxious to conserve. When traditions have been studied the focus has usually been on the transmission of texts. What is handed down in the form of a text within a culture is detached both from its producers and from any specific addressees, he says. A text can lead a life of its own, enjoying relative cultural autonomy. And yet we have assumed that such "inscribed" practices should be the privileged form for the transmission of a society's memories. We cannot underestimate the importance and persistence of the bodily aspects of social memory, he says, and suggests that every group will entrust to bodily automatisms the values they are most anxious to conserve.

What are the implications of this assertion? What are those daily practices, those bodily automatisms that embody the values we are most anxious to conserve? If as Mennonites, as Christians, we are experiencing a major shift in the practices that habituate our behaviors, what will our communities look like in twenty years?

Let me illustrate what I mean: I have been impressed of late with what an astounding quality kindness is. It used to sound like one of those wimpy virtues that were all about being nice. For anyone who wanted to make their mark in the world, kindness seemed more or less optional. But now I see things in a new light. Perhaps it is because rudeness has achieved raucous prominence by radio and TV talk show hosts and increasingly in daily discourse. Perhaps it is because selfishness seems more and more to be in the air and water all around us. For whatever multiplicity of reasons, I am blown away by simple acts of kindness.

It has been a frequent practice at our home to have Saturday evening cheese fondue. Several years ago (just after the Beijing summer Olympics) two young adult children came home for our Saturday evening fondue. Several of us had been travelling and missed the opening ceremonies for the Olympics. Our son regaled us with the story of the gigantic Chinese basketball star, Yao Ming, who led the Chinese team of athletes into the arena.

Beside him, holding his hand was a tiny, second grade boy—a survivor from the Sichuan quake zone. Not only had this little boy managed to crawl out of his collapsed school, he had also helped carry out two of his classmates. Our son reported that when asked why even though injured, he had gone back into the dangerous rubble to bring others out, the boy replied, "I was the hall monitor. It was my job to look after my school mates." After hearing this, we sat in stunned silence around the table. There is something that makes the heart sing when a gesture of courageous kindness steals the show on such a grand occasion. The fireworks were nice. The kindness of that boy was stupendous.

But what of more mundane kindness? I remember from growing up that there were acts of courtesy that had become pro forma, like guys opening doors for girls. Some of us scorned this gesture because we considered it a remnant of patriarchy. And in some ways it was. But now, when someone pushes through the door ahead of me and does not even notice I am there, I am reminded of how such small gestures schooled us on a daily basis to look out for another's interest above our own.

Oh, you say, what an exaggerated extrapolation to make from something as simple as holding a door open. Well, perhaps. But I know that I now often hold doors open for others in large part because of the courtesy shown me by those in my life who thoughtfully did so for me. This kindness does not need to be gender based, but to lose it because of gender politics is a great loss.

And whatever happened to table manners? I remember from family meals around the table little sayings like: "Mabel, Mabel strong and able. Get your elbows off the table. This is not a horse's stable." And other formative instructions: Be on time so you don't keep everyone else waiting. Wait to be seated until everyone has arrived. Bow your head for the table grace. Chew with your mouth closed. Wait to begin your dessert until everyone is served. Don't interrupt when someone else is talking. Take only your fair share so there's enough to go around. And carefully divide second helpings so everyone is taken into consideration.

Again, I know table etiquette can be painfully overdone. But consideration for others gathered around the table is evident in each of the illustrations above. Eating together can be a delightful communal experience, teaching us in small ways on a daily basis how to be respectful of others. As we share food with kind consideration for everyone around the table, mealtimes become formative in ways that extend far beyond the table. We experience goodness together at table and extend it in acts of hospitality beyond the table.

Why spend time on such mundane habits, or bodily automatism as Connerton calls them? How do they matter in the grandiose scheme of things? It is precisely with these little gestures that we train for the bigger things. With practice in ordinary routines, we may eventually learn to share food with the poor and welcome the outsider through the door. Sustained practice, over and over, with saying "I'm sorry," and "Please forgive me," teaches us to make peace with our enemy; to follow Jesus in all of life, to share the goodness of the Gospel.

Personal and communal practices are shared activities through which we come to form perspectives on reality and to know the truth as embodied by Jesus Christ. We get a better sense of what Jesus meant when he said: I am the way, the truth and the life.

Practices, when shaped in harmony with a comprehensive vision of the good, provide a coherent and sustained way of life; a way of "organizing goodness." Any community that wants to shape a quality life, a life that will counter mass culture with deeper, richer values, must reflect critically and creatively about what practices should characterize our life together.

## Conclusion

Just a few words in conclusion, on a Mennonite view of life and learning. How have we done on "practicing the way of Jesus?" Certainly, our track record is mixed—as it is for all faith communities. But let me offer the perspective of several dozen Mennonite affiliated young adults interviewed by a team I was working with on a research project:

One of the questions we asked was: Should the Mennonite Church continue to exist? I would summarize the response of the young adults we interviewed this way, excerpted from my book *Thank You for Asking: Conversing with Young Adults about the Future Church*.

Most of the interviewees said "yes," because the church has a distinct role to play both among other Christians and in the broader world: as an important voice in the world; a voice that needs to be heard more; as a community that offers an alternative way of living, seeing, interacting.

They described the special emphases that the Mennonite Church has to offer the world in various ways: peace and justice, a non-violent way of life, death penalty work, a social conscience to care for the poor and marginalized; a call to discipleship with a faith that impacts all that we do—our money, our job, our lifestyle. And there are other wonderful features these young adults associate with the Mennonite Church: "community" as a prominent and incredible strength; potlucks—including international potlucks; being globally minded; a wonderful heritage and sense of identity; hymn singing, living simply, washing feet, eating ethnic food; an open spirituality; a church that "becomes your family."

Hanan Alexander's asserts that "education is not first and foremost about acquiring knowledge, or gaining identity, or insuring group continuity . . . but rather about empowering a person to choose a vision of the good life."[6] The comprehensive vision of the good that fires my imagination as an educator and seminary president is a vision for God's shalom—made known to us in Jesus—who in his body made peace and created one new humanity, reconciled to God. Jesus, who proclaimed peace to those near and far, giving us access in one Spirit to God.

In gratitude, may we all daily offer ourselves to God in praise and thanksgiving. In joy and wonderment, may we seek to practice discipleship. With humility and forgiveness, may we learn together in family, with colleagues and fellow students, and in our congregations the goodness of abundant living. With courage and Spirit-imagination, may we witness to the good news of Christ's peace as central to God's grand comprehensive vision of good for the world.

## Bibliography

Alexander, Hanan. *Reclaiming Goodness: Education and the Spiritual Quest*. South Bend, IN: University of Notre Dame Press, 2001.

6. Alexander, *Reclaiming Goodness*, 9.

Bowman, Carl F., and Stephen L. Longenecker, eds. *Anabaptist Currents: History in Conversation with the Present*. Stonington, ME: Penobscot, 1995.

Connerton, Paul. *How Societies Remember*. Cambridge: Cambridge University Press, 1989.

Hays, Richard B. *The Moral Vision of the New Testament: A Contemporary Introduction to New Testament Ethics*. New York: HarperCollins, 1996.

Klassen, Walter. *Anabaptism in Outline: Selected Primary Sources*. Scottdale, PA: Herald, 1981.

Murray, Stuart. *The Naked Anabaptist: The Bare Essentials of a Radical Faith*. Scottdale, PA: Herald, 2010.

Yoder, John Howard. *The Politics of Jesus: Vicit Agnus Noster*. 2nd ed. Grand Rapids, MI: Eerdmans, 1994.

# CHAPTER SEVEN

# A Methodist View of Life and Learning:
# Conjoining Knowledge and Vital Piety

*W. Stephen Gunter*

IF ONE HOLDS THE "real" in tension with the "ideal," the scholar would perforce be required to place the Methodist ideal in an adversative construction: "Knowledge and Vital Piety: Joined and Disjoined in Methodist Higher Education." As with so many things called 'Methodist,' this conundrum of conjoining and disjoining has its origin in the brothers Wesley, John and Charles. Our story begins in the eighteenth century, in the summer of 1748, at a place called Kingswood in England's coal-mining district near Bristol. Like most other coal-mining centers, it was known mostly for its poverty, squalor, violence, and crime. It is well known that John Wesley, at George Whitefield's urging, first preached in the open air near Bristol, for the first time proclaiming the gospel message outside the consecrated space of a church pulpit, which he described as a "vile" practice. Less well known is that it was at this same time that Whitefield also urged upon Wesley the importance of his taking over the initiative that he himself had taken for a grammar school to educate coal miners' children in the Kingswood region. Whitefield's last act on April 2, 1739, on his way to board ship for an evangelistic mission to America, was to lay a foundation stone for the grammar school. He prayed that the powers of hell would not prevail against it. Just a few days before, March 29, 1739, he wrote in his journal: "It was surprising to see with what cheerfulness they [the miners] parted with their money [to build the school]. Were I to continue here, I would endeavor to settle schools all over the wood, . . . but I have only just time to set it on foot. I hope God will bless the ministry of my honored friend John Wesley, and enable him to bring it to good effect. It is a pity that so many little ones, as there are at Kingswood, should perish for lack of knowledge."[1]

Two points are striking in Whitefield's journal entry. First is the reference to the impoverished miners "cheerfully parting with their money" to build the school. The wages producing abject poverty assured that not a penny was superfluous to keeping body and soul together. The second noteworthy point is in the last line, "that so many little ones . . . should perish for lack of knowledge." Keep in mind that Whitefield was first, foremost, and always an evangelist, and when he talked about perishing, he was referencing eternal death. To modern ears this is a strange saying indeed, that children would suffer eternal death due to a "lack of knowledge" learned at school. But what is weird to us was perfectly normal to their ears, because such a saying was rooted in a widely held assumption that influenced both Whitefield and Wesley. Among the reigning intellectuals of their day, like the empiricist John Locke from a previous generation, the doctrine of original sin and the readily evident, pervasive nature of sin, even in young children, were believed, asserted, and emphasized in the most literal ways one might imagine. This dogma was connected to educational theory and practice, and philosophers like John Locke theorized that this human negation would be overcome through a strict and rigorous educational regimen.[2] Locke's pedagogy was connected to his vision for the progressive perfectibility of humanity. If children were placed very early under a rigorous educational regimen while they were still malleable and impressionable, and if this were done in successive generations, then the multiplying effects of education could counteract sin and eventually overcome its debilitating influence.

Wesley knew better than to rely totally on the educational process alone, but this philosophy of education was a foundational assumption at Kingswood School, even as it transitioned from being a school for local miners' children to being a proper residential boarding school. It remained rooted in charity for those who could not pay (such as Methodist itinerant preachers, whose children were non-paying), when Kingswood was officially chartered in 1748. John Wesley opened the school with a sermon based on Proverbs 22:6, "Train up a child in the way he should go, and

---

1. Whitefield, *George Whitefield's Journals*, 240.

2. Cf. Locke, *Thoughts Concerning Education;* and the ways John Wesley adopted Lockean assumptions in his "A Thought on the Manner of Educating Children," 474–77. See also, Trantor, "John Wesley and Education."

when he is old, he will not depart from it." Befitting the occasion, Charles Wesley composed a hymn "For Children":

Come, Father, Son, and Holy Ghost,
To whom we for our children cry!
The good desired and wanted most
Out of thy richest grace supply—
The sacred discipline be given
To train and bring them up to heaven.

Answer on them the end of all
Our cares, and pains, and studies here;
On them, recovered from their fall,
Stamped with the humble character
Raised by the nurture of the Lord,
To all their paradise restored.

Error and ignorance remove,
Their blindness both of heart and mind;
Give them the wisdom from above,
Spotless, and peaceable, and kind;
In knowledge pure their minds renew,
And store with thoughts divinely true.

Learning's redundant part and vain
Be here cut off, and cast aside;
But let them, Lord, the substance gain,
In every solid truth abide,
Swiftly acquire, and ne'er forego
The knowledge fit for man to know.

Unite the pair so long disjoin'd,
Knowledge and vital Piety:
Learning and Holiness combined,
And Truth and Love, let all men see,
In those whom up to thee we give,
Thine, wholly thine, to die and live.

Father, accept them through Thy Son,
And ever by thy Spirit guide!
Thy wisdom in their lives be shown,
Thy name confess'd and glorified;
Thy power and love diffused abroad,
Till all the earth is fill'd with God.[3]

Note the imbedded theological assumptions regarding depravity and the effects of education. Verse 1: "The sacred discipline be given, to train and bring them up for heaven." Verse 2: "Answer on them the end of all . . . On them, recovered from their fall, . . . Raised by the nurture of the Lord, To all their paradise restored." And then for our purposes here because of its permanent fixture in Methodist memory, verse 5:

Unite the pair so long disjoin'd,
Knowledge and vital Piety:
Learning and Holiness combined,
And Truth and Love, let all men see,
In those whom up to thee we give,
Thine, wholly thine, to die and live.

The most cited and recited couplet from this hymn, and perhaps any of Charles' poems, is: "Unite the pair so long disjoin'd, Knowledge and vital Piety." Interesting to note is that the phrase that follows, "Learning and Holiness combined," is seldom included in later Methodist references. Whether embedded in floor tiles, engraved in cornerstones, printed in catalogs or prominently displayed on campus signs, the reference is to connecting knowledge and piety. Richard Heitzenrater has aptly noted, "Commentary on this couplet is probably both overdone and undercooked, like a hamburger grilled over too hot a flame."[4] Even though the saying has been lifted up by Methodists, it has also been trod under foot—as is literally the case in Florence Hall (formerly the theology school, Kirby Hall) at Southern Methodist University where the engraved words are set in the hallway floor of marble and glass.[5] Lifted up and low, properly cited and misquoted,

3. Hymn 461 ("For Children"), "Come Father, Son, and Holy Ghost," in Wesley, *Works,* 9:643-44.

4. Heitzenrater, "Wesley and Education," 2.

5 Ibid., 9. Heitzernrater notes that it is misattributed to John Wesley rather than

this poetic phrase has defined Methodism's educational ideal for more the two and one half centuries; and this poetic couplet is especially pertinent to the theme of these Templeton Honors College lectures—"Liberal Arts and the Good Life." What did Charles Wesley's phrase imply originally, how has it played a role in Methodism's educational efforts, and how may it be creatively appropriated with integrity for the present day? Those questions entertain us in what follows.

The eighteenth century knew nothing of liberal arts nomenclature, as we employ the expression, but we got our inspiration from that era's pedagogy and curricula. In their day, an emphasis on learning languages began in earnest in elementary school, and that is why they were called grammar schools—only the grammar was Latin as well as English, and it began in the primary grades. John Wesley wrote and published five grammars for curricular use—English, Greek, Latin, German, and French. When we survey his Kingswood School curriculum, we encounter not only the languages, but also history, geography, chronology, rhetoric, logic, geometry, algebra, physics, music, ethics, astronomy, art, and reading the Christian Classics as well as Homer, Horace, Cicero, Tacitus, and Plato. English poetry focused on Spenser, Milton, and Shakespeare. Math and Science included the philosophy of Plato and the moderns: Locke, Malebranche and the *Philosophical Transactions*. "Wow," you say, "those are a lot of electives to choose from." Forget it! There were no electives for secondary school students; that was the 4-year curriculum that everyone followed.[6] Rather like the Honors College at Eastern University, Wesley called this his "course of academical learning," and asserted, "Whoever carefully goes through this course will be a better scholar than nine in ten of the graduates at Oxford or Cambridge."[7] In his "Plain Account of Kingswood School," he is even more bold: "If [Kingswood scholars] do not advance more here in three years than the generality of students at Oxford and Cambridge do in seven, I will bear the blame forever."[8] Such a rigorous curriculum certainly accounts for "knowledge" and "learning," but what about the equal emphasis on "holiness" and "vital piety" in Charles' hymn?

---

Charles, and it is also misquoted: "Let us unite the two so long divided."

6. This curriculum is outlined in Wesley's "Short Account of the School in Kingswood," 287–88.

7. Ibid., 389.

8. Ibid., 296.

There can be little doubt that for John and Charles, Christian pedagogy entailed the joining of knowledge and piety, wisdom and holiness. Even as we affirm this, we are left wondering what their conjoining might have meant to Methodists in later generations. Richard Heitzenrater suggests that the architecture of the Duke University Chapel comes closest to approximating the early Wesleyan understanding:

> At the back of the [Chapel] nave, in two niches under the Flentrop organ, are two statues that represent *Eruditio et Religio* . . . . The observer, however, cannot easily identify which statues represent which theme, since both look pious and both appear thoughtful. Wesley's understanding of knowledge and vital piety has the same sort of overlap. For him, knowledge is not a purely intellectual attribute but rather a channel of self-understanding, which is crucial for salvation. And vital piety entails not only a devotional stance based on love of God, but also a social outreach exemplified by love of neighbor.[9]

Wesley does not hesitate to repeat the maxim often attributed to St. Augustine, "Without love, all learning is but splendid ignorance." And could Wesley have expressed his sentiments more graphically than in his words to Bishop Lowth in 1780: "My Lord, I do by no means despise learning: I know the value of it too well . . . [but] what is a man that has [education but] no religion?" Then Wesley answers his own question, that education without true religion is little more than "a jewel in a pig's snout."[10]

Although Wesley was quite taken with certain Enlightenment empiricist emphases (as well as later Romanticists) and proceeded to make creative use of them,[11] he would have roundly rejected modern notions derived from the Enlightenment that require disinterested objectivity as a distinguishing characteristic of quality scholarship. Wesley's educational program involved the wholistic integration of body, mind, and spirit. Solid pedagogy pushed the boundaries of sin and ignorance, ever expanding the possibilities of what the student might know and become. Here he is in tune with the leading lights of his day asserting that self-knowledge is at

---

9. Heitzerater, "Wesley and Education," 10–11.

10. Wesley, *Works*, 13:143.

11. Cf. Cragg "Introduction," 1–36; Cragg, *Reason and Authority*; Brantley, *Locke, Wesley, and the Method of English Romanticism*; and Dreyer, "Faith and Experience in the Thought of John Wesley," 12–30.

the heart of a transformative educational process, for we must recognize that we are ignorant and sinful before we recognize any need for change.[12]

Wesley happily quotes William Law: "Education is to be considered as reason borrowed second hand, which is, as far as it can, supply the loss of original perfection."[13] Perfection, or holiness, for Wesley was pure love. This was made possible by a total reordering of fallen human nature, and educational pedagogy should be designed with this in view: "Education can thus be seen [for Wesley] as one means of grace by which the original perfection of creation (a creation of wisdom and holiness), lost in the Fall, could be restored."[14] It is not unfair to assert that in Wesley, and during at least the first one hundred fifty years of the Methodist educational vision after his demise, the goal of education was to a certain extent the same as the goal of religion. When pedagogy was properly construed and constructed, knowledge and vital piety, wisdom and holiness, learning and love are essentially linked. In almost every Methodist educational venue up to the beginning of the twentieth century, and still then on occasion in a few institutions, one encounters either a highly implicit or an explicit reference to linking knowledge and vital piety.

If the name Wesley was synonymous with early British Methodism, what name symbolized the heart and soul of American Methodism? Two alternatives present themselves: Thomas Coke and Francis Asbury. Both are remembered and revered, but the nod must go to Asbury, if for no other reason than that he refused to leave the colonies during the American Revolution—thereby winning the hearts of the citizens of the new republic. But there are other reasons as well, brilliantly and expansively described by John Wigger in his monumental biography of Asbury, *American Saint*.[15] America dwarfed England in size geographically, and Asbury's organization skills were up to the managerial challenges of expansive rural circuits that effectively brought the gospel to far-flung places. In 1771, when Asbury was commissioned by Wesley and arrived in America to oversee the work, there were a few hundred Methodists. In the year of Asbury's death, 1816, there were more than two hundred thousand Methodists. Put another way, in 1775 fewer than one out of every eight hundred Americans was a Method-

12. Cf. Body, *John Wesley and Education*, 49.

13. "On the Education of Children," 348, quoting from Law, *A Serious Call to a Devout Life*, a piece that Wesley abridged and published in 1744.

14. Heitzenrater, "Wesley and Education," 11.

15. Wigger, *American Saint*, 3–10.

ist; by 1812 Methodists numbered one out of every thirty-six Americans.[16] And keep in mind, this was also a time of explosive population growth. Asbury's leadership in this evangelistic endeavor was key, and no less than Wesley, Asbury believed that these converted souls needed education. A conversion experience alone was not accepted as adequate to complete the work of God—not for the individual and not for Methodism's eschatological vision for society.

The first Methodist college in America was chartered at the formal organizing of American Methodists as a church in 1784. Organizing the church and founding an educational center for Methodists went hand in glove. Named after Coke and Asbury, Cokesbury College's first president, Bishop John Fletcher Hurst, was inaugurated a few years later in 1787. In addition to the president, there were two other instructors and twenty-five students at the campus in Abingdon, Maryland. It is not an accident that the Methodist publishing arms are called Abingdon and Cokesbury. For all the success Methodists later had establishing schools, colleges, and universities, Cokesbury was not a permanent part of that success. Only one year after inaugurating its first president, the campus building burned in 1788, then it burned again in 1795; and when it burned to the ground on December 4, 1796, Cokesbury College ceased to exist. Asbury and Coke's dream for permanent institutions of higher education came after their death—Coke in 1814 and Asbury in 1816. Russell Richey records, "The General Conferences of 1820 and 1824 charged annual conferences with the establishment of schools, literary institutions, and colleges . . . . Gradually, [annual] conferences, often collaboratively, launched collegiate institutions, beginning with Augusta College in Kentucky (1822), Randolph-Macon in Virginia (1830), and Wesleyan University in Connecticut (1831)." The first women's college was chartered in 1836 as Wesleyan College in Macon, Georgia.[17] By the Civil War, "Methodism had established or was affiliated with some two hundred such collegiate institutions . . . . By one estimate Methodism succeeded in establishing thirty-four 'permanent' colleges before 1861."[18] Actually, the Methodist conviction about the importance of education led eventually to the establishment of more than 1,200 schools, only one in ten of which have survived into the twenty-first century.[19] Kingswood School and Charles Wes-

16. Ibid., 10.

17. Richey, "Connecting through Education," 206.

18. Cf. Tewksbury, *The Founding of American Colleges*, 103–11. Tewksbury estimates the Presbyterians founded forty-nine such "permanent" institutions (102).

19. Cunningim, *Uneasy Partners*, 10. Current membership of the National

ley's hymn were known to all, and the connection of knowledge and vital piety was at the heart of these early establishments. In support of this ideal, the early American Methodists poured their limited financial resources. Richey has noted, "On their behalf the emerging lay elites began to take leadership roles . . . [And in these institutions] the church equipped its ministry."[20] It is in this preparation for ministry that the connection of knowledge and vital piety is most evident, and that is the case almost without exception, even at Dickinson—chartered in 1784 by the 'Fathers of the Revolution,' but closely connected to Methodism from 1834 through the presidency of John P. Durbin and the financial sponsorship of the Philadelphia and Baltimore Annual Conferences. Schools like Dickinson in Pennsylvania, Wesleyan in Connecticut and Randolph-Macon in Virginia, among many others, served in effect as seminaries of their day. Their religion departments, populated by ordained ministers with degrees from the best institutions of their day, were in effect theology faculties. Stephen Olin, president of Wesleyan University in Connecticut, spoke for Methodism in 1844: "No Christian denomination can safely trust to others for the training of its sons . . . . History has too clearly demonstrated that, without colleges of our own, few of our sons are likely to be educated, and that only a small portion of that few are likely to be retained in our communion."[21]

In the light of Charles and John Wesley's sentiment about connecting knowledge and vital piety, we must not overlook questions about the nature of this Methodist educational enterprise. Opinions of scholars are mixed about whether there was a genuine consequential connection between faith and learning in the latter part of the nineteenth century. Some are of the opinion that the church had already lost "control" of its colleges by the period of the Civil War. Opinions range from sectarian to secular, depending on whether one reads Charles Seller's opinion about Dickinson after what he calls the "Methodist takeover,"[22] or James Scanlon's take on Randolph-Macon's early years to the effect that the college culture should

---

Association of United Methodist Schools and Colleges stands at 120, and several schools are deeply troubled financially.

20. Richey, "Connecting through Education," 208.

21. Olin, *The Works*, 2:249. It should be noted that almost all colleges at that time were not co-educational, and thus the education of sons and not daughters was all that was in view.

22. Sellers, *Dickinson College*, 195–99. Sellers sees Methodist involvement as a "sectarian takeover."

be characterized as more public and civic than pious.[23] David Potts' opinion on Wesleyan in Connecticut was much the same.[24] Glenn Miller flatly states, "These schools were more secular than the present-day observer might suppose from [reading] their presidents' rhetoric." But Miller also notes that the denominational colleges were a "curious hybrid" under the control of trustees accountable in some fashion to the denomination.[25]

Russell Richey drills through the tenor of these assessments as they related to Methodist colleges because, he asserts, they misunderstand the structure and culture of Methodism in this early period: "Those who minimize the Methodist character of the pre-Civil War college expect to find denominational control from some central agency or judicatory. For Methodists, such centralization did not exist."[26] Everybody was always on the move to accomplish evangelistic purposes. Annual Conferences, the primary sponsoring agencies, convened annually, but bishops actually rotated among them. Episcopal leadership was not stationary as it is today. In a real sense, everyone itinerated for the primary purpose of evangelization. Presiding elders, what we call district superintendents today, were appointed on the basis of evangelistic and missional effectiveness. As Richey points out, "The proof really came in the pudding. In substance, style, purpose, agenda, and ethos the colleges radiated Methodism. Not surprisingly, these schools in fact produced the church's leaders . . . . For the middle decades of the century, the stepping-stone to the episcopacy was a college presidency."[27] Of Wesleyan University's first forty years of graduates (919 through the decade of the Civil War), a third entered the Methodist ministry. Wesleyan University in Connecticut produced three quarters of the Methodist ministers who had college degrees.[28] Percentagewise we encounter a similar statistic at Randolph-Macon. Among the first two hundred and ten graduates, there were forty-three clergy, twelve of whom taught or served as college president. Other professions were also represented: forty-eight teachers (thirteen of these became professors in

23. Scanlon, *Randolph-Macon College*.

24. Potts, *Wesleyan University*.

25. Miller, *Piety and Intellect*, 127–39.

26. Richey, "Connecting through Education," 211.

27. Ibid., 212.

28. Duvall, *The Methodist Episcopal Church and Education*, 39–40.

one of the church's colleges), thirty-nine lawyers (eight of these became legislators), and twenty-nine physicians.[29]

As was the case for institutions of every type, the Civil War era was a watershed period for Methodism. In 1860, the General Conference had taken up the question whether annual conferences should continue to have primary control and supervision over the colleges and fledgling Methodist universities. Distinctions began to be made between the two types of institutions and their inherent intentionality. In work related to establishing a permanent Board of Education, a General Conference committee determined that "Annual Conferences would not consent to a transfer of the control of the 'literary institutions' under their care to the General Conference . . . nor [were] they sure, could this be done, that the educational movement of the church would not be robbed of much of its vitality . . . by attempting to direct it by a uniform and rigid system."[30]

If we try to formulate this worry in the words of this essay, it might come out in a question like this:

What are the related risks to keeping knowledge and vital piety conjoined when the grass roots connections to the church are severed and oversight is placed in distant hands? Although his research is not directed toward our specific question, Richey makes the pertinent observation: "By the late 1860s, Methodists recognized that vitality and freedom were being purchased at too high a price. Methodism had become too big, too complex, too institutionalized, and too wealthy to run itself by annual conferences that met only periodically . . . Hence, [what has been called] the revolution of 1872."[31] There was a concerted effort to bring all the educational institutions under the control of agencies established by the General Conference. A Board of Education had already been established in 1868 with loose definitions of authority, and it was determined that this would be the overseeing body of all colleges and universities. This move toward the general agency oversight led in 1892 to the creation of Methodism's University Senate. Indeed, it was in this entity that the Methodists established, the first of its kind in North America, a type of accrediting agency similar to what we have today in venues like North Central and the Southern Association of Colleges and Schools. This Methodist Senate served to establish academic standards, to apply them to individual institutions and to determine which

29. Cf. Scanlon, *Randolph-Macon College*, 56.

30. "Report of the Committee on Education," 390–91.

31. Richey, "Connecting through Education," 213.

schools qualified for formal recognition according to those standards. Qualifications also included an assessment of whether the school was authentically Methodist. Full endorsement from the Senate meant that supervising visits, counsel, and guidance would result in financial support.[32] Without exaggeration it can be asserted that the University Senate decided what counted as "Methodist" as well as what counted as quality education, and these two were inseparable in this early history. Eventually the overseeing agencies multiplied to oversee global Methodism's schools nationally and internationally. In addition to the University Senate, Methodism now has the General Board of Higher Education and Ministry, the National Association of United Methodist Schools and Colleges, and the Association of United Methodist Theology Schools—these latter two having no formal functions of assessment or funding responsibility. At the latest General Conference of 2012 in Tampa, it became clear that it is an open question whether it is any longer viable financially or missionally for the church to support such multiple layers of bureaucracy.

As is so often the case, finances drive the agenda, but the issue is fundamentally a missional one. While my comments to this point are fundamentally about organizational structure, the question must be asked, what is it, through the entire twentieth and now the twenty-first century, that fundamentally characterizes Methodist higher education? We have observed that from Wesley's era and basically through the entire nineteenth and into the twentieth century the essential nature was to hold together knowledge and vital piety. This was fundamentally what it meant to be authentically Methodist. As long as the connections to grass roots Methodism were strong, this dialectic was at work. In some places, of course, the constructive tension was greater than in others. This did not change immediately with the founding of the Methodist Senate at the end of the nineteenth century, but observable changes were in the wind. Methodism continued to establish colleges, and the nineteenth century witnessed also the establishment of institutions that were self-consciously different than the deeply church-connected colleges, namely universities. The Senate was charged with overseeing both, but if there was a difference between these two, what was that difference and how was it to be measured? Over a period of time it became apparent that the overriding characteristic difference was, in a word, "professionalism." Never mind that "profess" and "confess" are linguistically related. For Methodism the professionalism that began

32. Cf. Bowser, *Living the Vision*, 7–43.

with the establishment of the University Senate in 1892 took increasingly deep root. When institutional integrity became less and less defined at the more grass roots annual conference ministerial level, but rather at a distant organizational level, the question became, "Who populates the University Senate?" Initially, it was prominent ecclesial leaders, but as professionalism grew in American higher education, the credential of Senate members, and what they counted as having educational cash value, became increasingly tied to parallel organizations and bodies. Indeed, the church itself, with the requirement of a seminary degree for ordination, became increasingly professionalized. So, by the end of the twentieth century an Associate General Secretary of the Board of Higher Education could declare in my hearing at a college presidents' meeting, "Our Methodist colleges are church-related, not Christian!" This attribution could also be made in connection with several university-related schools of theology, as they operated more like schools of religious studies than seminaries intentionally connecting knowledge and vital piety. What actually happened during the twentieth century is that the preoccupation of gaining favor with professional credentialing from agencies outside the church, bodies increasingly hesitant about connecting piety and learning, led to full-blown secularity. The tendency has been to blame colleges and seminaries for this trend, but caution should be exercised on this issue. Tom Trotter reminds us: "The United Methodist Church, in a fit of distraction, passed a resolution in the 1968 General Conference that urged their colleges to consider separation from all church connections so that they would survive as independent secular institutions."[33] Trotter asserts that the question about church-related colleges and seminaries needs to be recomposed, "What is a college-related church?" When church-related and Christian could no longer be defined simply by dress codes, dances, and attending movies, the church was at a loss to know how to relate—having lost sight that it was St. Anselm who offered the maxim that became foundational to the entire western enterprise of education: *credo ut intelligam* (I believe in order that I might understand).[34]

Methodism's disjoining of knowledge and vital piety was not as simple as the church's forgetting a vital slogan. It came at the hand of a trinity of major influences: the financial role of Federal government requiring separation of church and state, the dominance of the Enlightenment model of the research university and its values, and the consequent displacement of

33. Trotter, "Introduction," 12.

34. Anselm of Canterbury, *Basic Writings*, 7.

the liberal arts idea as an integrative principle. With the loss of the liberal arts as an integrative principle, the marginalization of religion was essentially complete. Piety of any sort has been banished to student groups and chaplaincies. Methodist colleges may be church-related, but not Christian. As Russ Richey has so aptly observed: "These larger societal trends affecting higher education and the plight of the church college have been so overwhelming, have so dominated the consciousness of those in church and college leadership, and have so shaped our interpretive framework that we have tended to neglect the more insidious ways in which [they have] refashioned the relation of college to church."[35]

As Douglas Sloan and George Marsden have so eloquently argued, these tendencies represent more than just the loss of religiosity. More pernicious is the pervasive domination of an Enlightenment epistemology characterized by naturalism, Kantian dualism, rationalism, and materialism that reduces the whole of the spirit (aesthetic, ethical, and religious) to what can be observed and counted. Taken together, these eviscerate the spiritual innards of academic life. Given this spiritual wasteland, the well-intentioned are left grasping, as Sloan argues, for a qualitative mode of knowledge that would give faithful affirmation a foundation, or even a foothold, within the university.[36] Conrad Cherry has made the case that this is true to some extent in theological education in America as well—especially at university-related schools of theology, where it is intellectually less than respectable and certainly not sophisticated to connect knowledge and vital piety.[37] The culture of post-graduate schools of theology is slightly beyond the pale of our consideration in this essay, but one must be careful lest we forget that it is the secular university culture that dictates the norms of professionalism. Learned societies do not look to the culture of church-related, Christian colleges to determine the standards for what has cash value in the academic guilds. To maintain an educational culture that values the connection between knowledge and vital piety is not an undertaking for the faint of heart, for it requires swimming against the tidal flow of established non-belief.

The call to "reform the nation and the church" was a dual emphasis for Methodism in America that went hand in glove with connecting knowledge and vital piety. This vision could not be accomplished by religious

---

35. Richey, "Connecting through Education," 219.

36. Cf. Marsden, *The Soul of the American University*; and Sloan, *Faith and Knowledge*.

37. Cf. Cherry, *Hurrying Toward Zion*.

enthusiasm and piety alone, because the church did not see itself simply as one among many other social institutions. The church lived out of and into an eschatological vision that entailed the comprehensive improvement of society. Increasingly the privatization of religion has moved the church to the margins of societal change. Even a cursory reading of Western civilization will reveal that most of the great reformations have begun in educational settings, but this happened in a context where faith and learning were inextricably intertwined.[38] As the church has been in the process of forgetting this historic nexus, it has also been tacitly and even at times explicitly encouraging the state to assume responsibility for social services and societal change—thereby relegating itself to marginal significance in societal transformation. I doubt that the organized church in North America, especially in its mainline manifestations, has the capacity to reverse itself on this score, but I would assert that historically church-related institutions do, in fact, possess the capacity for transformational change. It has been suggested that going forward in this connection, it will be the educational institutions who will need to be the "active senior partner."[39] To accomplish this will require a monumental effort of institutional will, for the supreme importance of secular guild values and the emphasis on professional prestige undergirding those societies does not fit easily or well with the dialectic of faith and learning, what in historic Methodist parlance is called knowledge and vital piety. Faith seeking understanding is not a new idea, but its remembrance and practice is seriously threatened, even in church-related educational institutions.

We hear a lot these days about "teaching values."[40] The prior question goes begging, "On the basis of what grounds do we define a value?" How

38. In his yet to be published McDonald Lecture, "Universities and Movements of Christian Transformation," delivered at Oxford (May, 2012), Harvard Divinity Dean, David Hempton, notes three such major movements: (1) Ignatius of Loyola, The Society of Jesus, at the University of Paris in the 1530s; (2) August Hermann Francke, the Pietists, at Halle University in the 1690s; (3) John and Charles Wesley, Methodism, at Oxford University in the 1730s.

39. Cunningim, *Uneasy Partners*. This assertion is the fundamental premise and essential conclusion of Cunningim's book.

40. Ibid., 120. Cunningim's *ad hominen* assertion (pp. 70–71) that what Marsden, *The Soul of the American University*, argues for is "his set of values" misses the mark as well as the point. Marsden is making the case that the essential values that Cunningim want to argue for, especially in church-related institutions, has been banished from the intellectual's vocabulary. That world of faith, virtue and value that this language enshrined has been lost—and with it the loss of the interconnected reality.

do we teach values when efforts to instill virtue are increasingly Balkanized as narrow-minded indoctrination? For more than five hundred years in western institutions of higher education, religion and faith played the role of defining value orientation. During the last half of the twentieth century, most colleges and universities did their dead level best to confine classroom education to the life of the mind—as if this could be disconnected from an embodied self. So even when "teaching values" are offered, there is little to inform what that actually means other than "do good" and "be good." The prior value orientation question still goes largely begging, left to that which is construed to be civic-minded. So successive generations of civic-minded students have been taught to do some civic good along their merry head-long way, drinking the Koolaid (among other cool beverages) that the most important thing their college degree could do for them was guarantee a good job and lifestyle at least as good as that of their parents—and that immediately upon graduation. I am reminded of the words of our family physician in Atlanta, who also taught at the Emory University School Medicine. She and her physician partner had gone to three-quarters time for reasons of quality of life and quality of patient care, versus amount of annual income: "The difference between me and most students I teach in medical school is this, I am satisfied with making a living; they are determined to make a fortune."

Richard Heitzenrater reminds us, "Values or virtues have obvious models, specific moorings, and particular implications. 'The good' is more than a lack of evil." [41] The absence created by evil is at best a mere vacuum, and at its worst a comprehensively destructive force that can only be overcome by a fundamental reorientation capable of filling and transforming the void. In Christian theology that fundamental orientation is transcending love—love to God and neighbor that flows from redemptive transformation into societal transformation. This brings us back to the Augustinian maxim, "All learning without love is but splendid ignorance." In Wesleyan poetic shorthand, the elegance of splendid learning invariably connects knowledge and vital piety. May they once again be conjoined in church-related institutions of higher education. If this should occur, then our graduates will be connected to living a good life, rather than simply making a good living. And who knows but that God's eschatological vision for our world might yet reappear in our line of sight.

41. Heitzenrater, "Wesley and Education," 12.

# Bibliography

Anselm of Canterbury, *Basic Writings*. Translated by S. N. Deane, with intro by Charles Hartshorne. LaSalle, IL: Open Court, 1964.

Body, Alfred H. *John Wesley and Education*. London: Epworth, 1936.

Bowser, Beth Adams. *Living the Vision: The University Senate of the Methodist Episcopal Church, the Methodist Church, and the United Methodist Church, 1892–1991*. Nashville: United Methodist Church Board of Education, 1992.

Brantley, Richard E. *Locke, Wesley, and the Method of English Romanticism*. Gainesville: University Press of Florida, 1984.

Cherry, Conrad. *Hurrying Toward Zion: Universities, Divinity Schools, and American Protestantism*. Bloomington: Indiana University Press, 1995.

Cragg, Gerald R. "Introduction." In *The Appeals to Men of Reason and Religion and Certain Related Open Letters*, vol. 11 of *The Works of John Wesley (The Bicentennial Edition)*, 1–36. Nashville: Abingdon, 1987.

———. *Reason and Authority in the Eighteenth*. Cambridge: Cambridge University Press, 2013.

Cuningim, Merrimon. *Uneasy Partners: The College and the Church*. Nashville: Abingdon, 1995.

Dreyer, Frederick. "Faith and Experience in the Thought of John Wesley." *American Historical Review* 88 (February 1983) 12–30.

Duvall, Sylvanus M. *The Methodist Episcopal Church and Education up to 1869*. New York: AMS Press, 1928.

Heitzenrater, Richard. "Wesley and Education." In *Methodism and Education: From Roots to Fulfillment*, edited by Sharon J. Hels, 1–13. Nashville: General Board of Higher Education and Ministry, 2000

Locke, John. *Thoughts Concerning Education*. Mineola, NY: Dover, 2007.

Marsden, George. *The Soul of the American University: From Protestant Establishment to Established Nonbelief*. New York: Oxford University Press, 1994.

Miller, Glenn T. *Piety and Intellect: The Aims and Purposes of Ante-Bellum Theological Education*. Atlanta: Scholars, 1990.

Olin, Stephen. *The Works of Stephen Olin, D.D., LL.D., Late President of Wesleyan University*. New York: Harper, 1853.

Potts, David B. *Wesleyan University, 1831–1910: Collegiate Enterprise in New England*. New Haven, CT: Yale University Press, 1992.

"Report of the Committee on Education appointed by the General Conference of 1860." In *Journals of General Conference: Methodist Episcopal Church*.

Richey, Russell. "Connecting through Education." In *Doctrine in Experience: A Methodist Theology of Church and Ministry*, 201–224. Nashville: Kingswood, 2009.

Scanlon, James Edward. *Randolph-Macon College: A Southern History, 1825–1967*. Charlottesville: University of Virginia Press, 1983.

Sellers, Charles C. *Dickinson College: A History*. Middletown: Wesleyan University Press, 1973.

Sloan, Douglas. *Faith and Knowledge: Mainline Protestantism and American Higher Education*. Philadelphia: Westminster John Knox, 1994.

Tewksbury, Donald G. *The Founding of American Colleges and Universities Before the Civil War*. New York: Teacher's College, Columbia University, 1932.

Trantor, Donald. "John Wesley and the Education of Children." In *Issues in Education: Some Methodist Persepctives*, 15–40. Oxford: Applied Theology Press, 1996.

Trotter, Thomas F. "Introduction." In *Uneasy Partners: The College and the Church*, Merrimon Cuninggim, [AQ: page range?]. Nashville: Abingdon, 1995.

Wesley, John. "On the Education of Children." In *Sermons III (71–114)*, vol. 3 of *The Works of John Wesley (The Bicentennial Edition)*, 348. Nashville: Abingdon, 1986.

———. "Short Account of the School in Kingswood." In *Doctrinal and Controversial Treatises II*, vol. 13 of *The Works of John Wesley (The Bicentennial Edition)*, 287–88. Nashville: Abingdon, 2013.

———. "A Thought on the Manner of Educating Children." In *Doctrinal and Controversial Treatises II*, vol. 13 of *The Works of John Wesley (The Bicentennial Edition)*, 474–77. Nashville: Abingdon, 2013.

———. *The Works of John Wesley.* 14 volumes. Edited by Thomas Jackson. Reprint of 1872 Wesleyan Conference Office Edition. Kansas City: Beacon Hill, 1958.

Whitefield, George. *George Whitefield's Journals.* Edinburgh: Banner of Truth Trust, 2007.

Wigger, John. *American Saint: Francis Asbury and the Methodists.* Oxford: Oxford University Press, 2012.

# Epilogue

*Phillip Cary*

IT LOOKS LIKE WE have a problem with Protestant activism. By that I mean the Protestant turn away from the contemplative ideal, which has been central to the life of the mind in the West since Plato and which was well represented in the *vita contemplativa* of the middle ages. If activism is a kind of ailment, then American evangelicalism has a particularly bad case of it. Yet we may hope that what makes it so bad in this case has less to do with Protestant theology than with the pressure to appeal to consumers in the spiritual marketplace of modern America. If such hope does not disappoint us, then a renewed attention to theological traditions with roots older than consumerism might teach us a thing or two, especially about how to do the work of education in the liberal arts. That at any rate is the hope that moved the editors, both of whom are my colleagues at an evangelical Christian university, to assemble the essays in this volume.

They have presented the essays in roughly chronological order, according to the age of the tradition each one represents. Roughly, I say. The roughness smoothes out a bit if we take the essay on Eastern Orthodoxy to have its home base in the church fathers and the essay on Roman Catholicism to be grounded in the achievements of medieval thought. (Let's not try to adjudicate between Orthodoxy and Catholicism when it comes to claims of priority). What the chronological order displays is a kind of nearness to the ancient Platonist ideal of contemplation in Orthodoxy and Catholicism, compared to something more distant from ancient thought in the essays at the end, where a Mennonite and a Methodist present versions of Protestant activism. In the middle are three essays that might show us something about why Protestantism turned away from ancient contemplation to a distinctive kind of activism.

The question in my mind is what wisdom there is in Protestant activism and its distance from ancient contemplation. It is a question that brings us back—as always in Western thought—to Plato, who invented the very idea of the liberal arts and connected them from the beginning with the experience of contemplation. The preface to this volume reminds us of his vivid and extraordinarily influential way of illustrating this connection: it is like ascending out of a cave of shadows and into the light of the supreme Good, a turning or conversion from the realm of appearances to a contemplative intellectual vision of true reality, which is divine. We must learn to doubt the shadows, Plato teaches, because they represent not only the superficial appearances of the visible world but the sophistry woven into the active life of political opportunism, the game played by prisoners of the cave, who offer rewards—honor and money and power—to those who succeed best at naming the shadows. Liberal education, by contrast, gets people turned around to see the light of truth—seeing it for themselves, not just giving the right answer on a test—for without such vision they remain captive to the shadows, driven by "the heavy pressure for results" described by Mark Noll in the words quoted in the Introduction. This education is called liberal because it is for free people, those who must see for themselves what justice is if they are to bear the burdens of civic responsibility, and who must begin to develop real wisdom if they are to live a good life. From a Christian perspective, such education is clearly a work of love—for love seeks the good of the neighbor, and it is a great good in the lives of young people to learn to see the truth for themselves.

So it is a real problem if Protestant activism means giving up contemplation altogether, and the longing which desires wisdom for its own sake. "The beginning of wisdom is this: get wisdom," says the biblical proverb, "and whatever you get, get understanding" (Prov 4:7). It is not just that our activist projects to change the world are likely to fail if we don't take the trouble to know what we're doing. It is that we fail to love our students if we educate them only as "change agents," tools for our agendas of social transformation, experts at naming the shadows but unacquainted with wisdom and the good life. For as another proverb puts it, wisdom "is a tree of life to those who get hold of her." (Proverbs 3:14) To promote an education without love of wisdom is a sin, contrary to the love of neighbor and the biblical commandment to choose life (Deut 30:19).

"But where shall wisdom be found?" as the good man asked (Job 28:12). The Christian answer cannot be quite the same as Plato's, because what Christian faith ultimately desires to contemplate is a quite distinctive divine reality, the Father who gives us his own Son in human flesh so that we may know him through his own Spirit. The nature and consequences of that distinctive contemplation afford us a kind of thread to follow as we move from the more ancient to the more modern Christian traditions represented in this book.

1. James Carey's essay on Eastern Orthodoxy identifies the core of Christian contemplation as a theological *noesis*, using the Platonic-Aristotelian word for what mind does (rendered *intellectus* in Latin, and understanding or intuition in English) when it does more than merely reason discursively, moving logically from one step to another as we figure things out. Reason indeed is something precious, for more than anything else it is reason (*logos*) that constitutes in us the image of God, who has his own precious Logos, the eternal word and reason by which he made and redeems all things (John 1:1–18). Yet the movement of our reason is insufficient without the prior movement of the divine Logos who becomes flesh for our sake in Jesus Christ. Hence the vision of the supreme Good and Truth and Beauty is not impersonal, but is a theological *noesis* moving us in an infinite progress towards the triune God who elevates us into participation in his own nature. It is clear that something more than intellectual vision is involved in the Christian notion of contemplation.

2. R. J. Snell, presenting a Roman Catholic vision of education, interestingly shies away from the metaphor of vision. He does not invoke the classic Thomistic description of the chief end of man as beatific vision, the intellectual seeing of God, which makes us eternally happy. Yet he does not abandon the contemplative life, but on the contrary sees it as the ground and source of the active life of work and learning. The contemplative life in turn, with its love and delight and knowledge, is grounded in the self-communication of the divine life: the Father giving being to the Son, and Father and Son together giving being to the Spirit, a giving which freely spills over in the sheer gift of creation and the yet deeper gift of redemption. The fact that vision is not quite the right metaphor for what it is like to be on the receiving end of this divine self-communication is suggested by Bernard Lonergan, the twentieth-century Catholic thinker who is at the center of much of Snell's own scholarship.[1] For Lonergan, human knowing can't be like "just taking a look." It requires more than vision and understanding,

---

1. See especially Snell, *Through a Glass Darkly.*

but must proceed to the discursive judgments of reason, which are precisely its means of access to reality, its opportunity to say: "it is so." This may seem like collapsing intuitive and discursive reason, but it would be better to say it is an account of *noesis* that gets us beyond Plato's ocular metaphor. It affords us a modern version of the Aristotelian-Thomist view of knowledge as forming the soul. To know is not just to see the form of things at a distance but to take on the form of what is known—as if, to use the biblical metaphor, it were written on the heart. That is why, in Snell's Catholic account, the contemplation of divine beauty is at the foundation of everything. Everything else, including the active life of work and justice, follows from the way the knowledge of God as beauty forms us in love and delight.

3. In Lutheran theology, the name for this formation is faith. In his lectures on Romans, Luther teaches that "there is a similar form of the Word and the believer," and in his lectures on Galatians he speaks of the Christ himself as "the form of our faith," so that believers "have the same form in their mind that God or Christ has."[2] We are justified by faith alone because only the Gospel word has the power to form Christ in us. Since faith comes by hearing, and hearing by the word of Christ (Rom. 10:17), the Lutheran form of contemplation is to hear the Gospel. In place of Plato's ocular metaphor we have something more like music forming our hearts, like a favorite song or story in which we find ourselves. The formative power of the Gospel underlies the theology of the two kingdoms that Korey D. Maas, in his essay, uses to articulate a distinctively Lutheran view of the place of liberal education. Like Plato, Luther sees the liberal arts as necessary for a just and healthy civic order. But in addition, the liberal arts contribute to the kingdom of Christ by sharpening the skills of reading and speaking and singing needed to take hold of the word of God and teach it. So liberal education serves Christ as he gives form to our hearts through his word. This in turn is the source of Protestant activism. Once the Gospel frees us from the anxious need to justify ourselves, it leaves us no work to do but to serve our neighbor. Thus in the famous paradoxical formulation of Luther's *Freedom of a Christian*, Christians are both free and slaves at the same time: free lords of all, liberated

2. See Luther's comment on Rom 3:7 in AE 25:211, and his comments on Gal 2:16 and 4:20 in AE 26:130 and 431. (AE = American Edition of Luther's Works, cited by Maas in footnote [x-REF], cf., expanded citation in Maas bibliography.)

from sin and death, and yet dutiful servants of all, subject to their neighbors. For once Christ has given himself to us in faith, there is no work left for us to do but to give ourselves in love to others. What drops out of the picture here is not only the metaphor of intellectual vision but also Plato's metaphor of ascent. The Beloved, the supreme Good in person, has already descended and given himself to all who believe, like a bridegroom who has promised himself to his bride. This good news has ample room for comfort and joy as well as works of love for the world, but no place for a spirituality in which love is our way to God. It turns out, that is not what love is for.

4.  Mennonite seminary president Sara Wenger Shenk speaks for a tradition that habitually thinks much more of action than of contemplation. The focus is on a community that seeks to "organize goodness" by following Jesus. Yet I notice a number of similarities with the other traditions represented in this volume. She too thinks in terms of formation, about identifying so closely with the life and practices of Jesus that "one's life is shaped by that life." She too sees the Gospel as the story of Christ, which the whole community indwells by means of bodily practices as well as by reading and interpreting Scripture together. Because Anabaptists learn Christ's story by living it out in communal *practices*, they seldom insist on a sharp contrast between faith and works. Yet if we adopt Luther's definition of the Gospel as focusing on what Christ does (received in faith), in contrast to the Law which focuses on what we do (actualized in good works), then the Gospel is clearly at the foundation of her "vision for God's shalom—made know to us in Jesus—who in his body made peace and created one new humanity, reconciled to God." Here too faith comes before works: prior to the work of following Jesus is the good news of Christ's peace as the basis of the good life for the whole world. There is no explicit account of contemplation here, but there is something higher and prior to our activism, to which an education for shalom must continually return.

5.  It is typical of the Reformed to be epistemologically ambitious, to insist that reason serve faith and that all knowledge as well as culture be shaped by Christian convictions. In the Dutch Reformed tradition that formed Esther Lightcap Meek, this means that the Gospel receives the philosophical ministrations of a whole worldview and its presuppositions. But Meek is concerned that the worldview approach

may be too fond of what Abraham Kuyper called the *antithesis* between Christian culture and the secular world. The problem is not that Christ claims anything less than the whole world, but that the concept of worldview has a distinctively modern and rationalist pedigree, too inclined to define knowledge abstractly as if it consisted only in having the right views about the world, which means it fails to fully "invite the real." Hence also it fails to fully engage the whole of embodied, social, hermeneutical selves, and thus leaves out too much of how we learn and love to know. Meek's own covenant epistemology harnesses insights from philosopher Michael Polanyi to provide an alternative, which resonates most deeply with the previous essays when it takes the paradigm of knowing to be "the redemptive encounter, enacted in the Eucharist." This is what I would take to be a properly Christian account of contemplation, a foretaste of the consummation of all things in which, as the Westminster Shorter Catechism puts it, we "glorify God and enjoy him forever."

6. The Reformation Anglicanism described by Ashley Null shares the distinctively Protestant understanding of the Gospel as the word and story of Christ, and sets it in the context of worship. In Null's wonderful analogy, it is as if God had nothing better to do than spend hours and hours telling us his story, so that at the end we can get up and dance knowing who it is who loves us. Yet the more you look at it, the less distinctively Protestant this looks, and the more it seems to be what good Christian liturgies have been doing all along. Here—as with Lutheranism also—we have two ways of forming the soul, feeding it with both word and sacrament. So it is no surprise that Anglicanism has always been open to a high church traditionalism, as is evident especially in nineteenth-century Anglo-Catholicism. Many of our evangelical students at Eastern University are attracted to Anglican worship precisely because of its piety of word and sacrament, where the Gospel is not a technique we use to get saved, but is Christ giving himself to us in external words and signs every Sunday, so that we may feed on him in our hearts by faith, with thanksgiving.

7. The educational vision of Methodism—a tradition deeply imbued with Protestant activism—is often summarized, W. Stephen Gunter informs us, in lines from a Charles Wesley hymn asking God to "unite the pair so long disjoined, knowledge and vital piety." The history of Methodist higher education that Gunter sketches for us culminates

in the story of how these two have gradually come apart. It is a story that is hardly confined to Methodism, as George Marsden and others have shown. From our standpoint in the Templeton Honors College at Eastern University, it is a story from which we would like to learn some lessons—especially, how to resist the social and cultural forces that pull these two apart and result in the secularization of once-Christian universities. One lesson, clearly, is to honor professional academic standards without letting them dictate our vision of the good of education. But I'm thinking another lesson is suggested by the next two lines of the hymn, which goes on to pair "learning and holiness" as well as "truth and love." A purely activist reading of that last pair would put truth at the service of love of neighbor. But surely we must begin with a more contemplative reading that would form us in love of truth for its own sake. In the non-Platonist form that I have been suggesting, this means a joyous reception of the truth in person, Christ the Beloved given to us in the word of the Gospel, "in whom are hidden all the treasures of wisdom and knowledge" (Col. 2:3). Whenever Protestant activism forgets to love and contemplate the truth of the Gospel, it gets cut off from its roots.

So here is what I propose we can learn by setting the essays on these seven traditions side by side. First of all, everything begins with God's good gift, which begins with himself. The life of learning can never do more than circle back to this gift, even when it is simply learning the ways of God's creation in one of the so-called "secular" disciplines. To do less than this is to try making our activism into the ultimate source of the good, and that can at best be failure and at worst idolatry. We will surely see enough in the years to come of human beings trying to define their own good by their own activity. Christian education must stand as a witness to a better good than can be achieved by our activism or defined by our efforts, a good we can only receive with gratitude and await with longing (even so, come Lord Jesus) and in the meantime must obey in our active lives.

And therefore we must learn. We must educate ourselves and our students in the good that is the ground of our activism because it is prior to our activism. Our various traditions may call this grounding by the name of faith in the Gospel, love of truth, following Jesus, feeding the soul, forming the heart, contemplating the Good, or participating in the triune life of God, but however we call it, our educational work cannot do without it. Yet by the same token, our various traditions cannot continue as traditions—as the active handing down of wisdom known originally as *traditio*—without the work of teaching and education that forms young people in the life of the tradition, so that their hearts are formed in the image of the good to which the tradition is devoted. Because of this good, we have good work to do.

## Bibliography

Snell, R. J. *Through a Glass Darkly: Bernard Lonergan and Richard Rorty on Living without a God's-eye View*. Milwaukee: Marquette University Press, 2006.

Made in the USA
San Bernardino, CA
18 September 2015